The Journal of Entrepreneurial Finance

Spring 2013 Volume 16 No. 2

The Journal of Entrepreneurial Finance

The Journal of Entrepreneurial Finance is the official publication of the Academy of Entrepreneurial Finance, which is a division of the Academy of Behavioral Finance & Economics

www.aobf.org

P.O. Box 157
Montrose, CA 91021-0157, USA

The Journal of Entrepreneurial Finance

Spring 2013 | Volume 16 | No. 2

Library of Congress ISSN 1551-9570

Disclaimer

The Editor of the Journal of Entrepreneurial Finance (JEF) is responsible for deciding which of the research papers/articles submitted to the journal should be published. The publishing decision is based on the recommendation of the journal's reviewers. The Editor may be guided by the policies of the journal's editorial board and constrained by such legal requirements as shall then be in force regarding libel, copyright infringement and plagiarism. The Editor may confer with other editors or reviewers in making this decision.

The publisher, the Academy of Entrepreneurial Finance, the Academy of Behavioral Finance & Economics, and the editors cannot be held responsible for any errors or consequences arising from the publication of the content in this journal. The views and opinions expressed herein reflect those of the authors only, and do not necessarily reflect those of the above organizations or the editors.

The Journal of Entrepreneurial Finance

Spring 2013 | Volume 16 | No. 2

TABLE OF CONTENTS

THE JOURNAL OF ENTREPRENEURIAL FINANCE VOLUME 16, NO. 2 (SPRING 2013) 1-32

Operationalizing a Behavioral Finance Risk Model: A Theoretical and Empirical Framework

Rassoul Yazdipour, Ph.D.
California State University and
The Academy of Behavioral Finance & Economics

William P. Neace, Ph.D.
Health Care Excel

ABSTRACT

To keep up with the rather fast-growing interest in the discipline of Behavioral Finance and Economics – caused in part by the new realities of the post-2008 world, and the realities prevailing over three decades before and leading up to that year– there is a discernible need for the production of new generations of testable and yet more realistic models and theories as guides for financial and economic decision makers everywhere. The present work is one such attempt in that direction. This writing first improves upon a recently developed, and real-life-inspired, Behavioral Finance Risk Model (Yazdipour, 2011) and then offers a specific methodology for testing it.

JEL Classification: D81, G39, M13
Keywords: Behavioral Finance, Behavioral Economics, Risk and uncertainty, Risk Model

I. Introduction and a Review of the Literature

A REVIEW OF THE LITERATURE ON PERCEIVED RISK provides the needed backdrop for presenting the Behavioral Finance Risk Model (BFRM) as presented and used in this writing. Both the extant literature and the related methodologies will be discussed as follows.

 ISSN: 1551-9570.
This article is reprinted from the Journal of Behavioral Finance & Economics, Vol.3

A. The Literature on Perceived Risk

Early literature examining perceived risk suggested that risk is multidimensional (e.g., Bauer, 1967; Bettman, 1973; Cunningham, 1967; Roselius, 1971; Jacoby & Kaplan, 1972; Zikmund & Scott, 1973). As such, *perceived risk* may be distinguished from traditional economic conceptualizations of *risk* as a statistical property (e.g., as outcome probability or variance of a probability distribution over outcomes) within the dominant Expected Utility framework (e.g., Johnson, 2004; Froot, Scharfstein, & Stein, 1993; Ganzach, 2000; Jorgensen & Kirschenheiter, 2003; Mitchell, 1999; Weber, Anderson, & Birnbaum, 1992). Many scholars have treated risk as a perception rather than as an objective statistical property, and have defined it in terms of peoples' reports about the "riskiness" associated with given choice alternatives or their evaluations of "riskiness" for a given set of behaviors (e.g., Ganzach, Ellis, Pazy, & Ricci-Siag, 2008; Pollatsek & Tversky, 1970; Sitkin & Weingart, 1995; Weber, Blais, & Betz, 2002; Weber & Milliman, 1997; for a thorough discussion of risk as perception, see Olsen, in press). Although there is no universally agreed upon definition of perceived risk in the literature (see Mitchell, 1999, for a review of definitions of perceived risk in the consumer behavior literature, and Conchar, Zinkhan, Peters, & Olavarrieta, 2004, for a broad review of definitions of perceived risk across the marketing, psychological, finance, economics, and related literatures), it can be generally conceived of as a psychological property associated with three common but not mutually exclusive elements of a decision situation. The first element is uncertainty over outcomes, which may be represented by notions of "chance," or by objective or subjective probability estimates. The second element is importance of the consequences, and is closely related to the third element, which is the potential for loss or perception of unpleasant consequences associated with a set of choice alternatives (e.g., Bettman, 1973; Conchar et al., 2004; Cunningham, 1967; Kogan & Wallach, 1964; Peter & Tarpey, 1975; Swait & Erdem, 2007; Mitchell, 1999; Weber et al., 2002; Ganzach, 2000; Ganzach et al., 2008).

An influential line of research in the area of perceived health and technological risks further solidified perceived risk as a psychological variable through the formulation of a set of seven "psychological risk dimensions" (Slovic, 1987; Slovic, Fischhoff, & Lichtenstein, 1986). In contrast to traditional economic risk conceptualizations, the psychological risk dimensions incorporate more global evaluations of choice alternatives in what some researchers consider to be a top-down evaluation process of forming perceptions and making judgments in general (e.g.,

Bargh, 1997; Ledoux, 2000; Zajonc, 1998). Among Slovic's (1987) seven psychological risk dimensions are items related to an affective evaluation of risky prospects, such as "dread" (degree to which negative consequences of the risky prospect are feared or anxiety-provoking), and "catastrophic potential" (perceived worse-case disaster severity of the risky prospect).

More recently, a number of researchers have further explored the affective nature of judgment and choice (e.g., Bechara, Damasio, & Damasio, 2000; Kahneman, 2003; Loewenstein, Weber, Hsee, & Welch, 2001; Mellers, Schwartz, Ho, & Ritov, 1997), and provide substantial evidence for an affect-based evaluative component in judging perceived risk. Findings such as the perceived negative relationship between risk and benefit (Finucane, Alhakami, Slovic, & Johnson, 2000; Ganzach, 2000; Slovic, Finucane, Peters, & MacGregor, 2004), and the relative insensitivity of judgments to outcome probabilities for emotionally powerful stimuli (Rottenstreich & Hsee 2001) are seen as evidence for an "Affect Heuristic" (Slovic, Finucane, Peters, & MacGregor, 2002) in which risk judgments proceed from a global assessment of a prospect as "good or bad."

A related line of research argues that uncertainty produces an elevated level of negative affect, or "psychological discomfort," and that decision-makers are motivated to reduce their discomfort by taking actions to reduce inherent uncertainty in the situation (Neace, Deer, Michaud, & Bolling, 2011). Thus, in addition to three common elements of perceived risk, some scholars have added controllability, manageability, and confidence in estimates of the extent to which uncertainty can be controlled or otherwise managed through the acquisition of information or the application of skill/experience (e.g., March & Shapira, 1987; Baird & Thomas, 1985; Sitkin & Weingart, 1995; Sitkin & Pablo, 1992). Choices may then follow from a desire to reduce uncertainty (e.g., Cho & Lee, 2006; Huber et al., 2001; Lipshitz & Strauss, 1997; Neace, Deer, & Barnard, 2010) in order to reach and maintain an individual level of comfort with it (Konopka & Ackley, in press), suggesting individual differences in perceived risk tolerance.

Indeed, an impressive body of evidence indicates that risk perception is not a stable trait across people or situations, further distinguishing it from traditional statistical definitions offered by the EU framework. Risk perception has been found to differ from individual to individual, for the same individual across different situations, across different contexts and domains, in different problem frames, and across cultures (Bontempo, Bottom, & Weber, 1997; Cooper, Wu, & Dunkelberg, 1988; Ferguson &

Gallagher, 2007; Holtgrave & Weber, 1993; MacCrimmon & Wehrung, 1990; Sitkin & Weingart, 1995; Weber, 1988; Weber et al., 1992; Weber et al., 2002). For example, Weber et al. (2002) found that the degree of risk taking was domain specific, and that people's behaviors were not consistently risk-seeking or risk-averse across financial, health and safety, recreational, ethical, and social decisions. They suggested that risk perception is a state rather than a trait characteristic, and that it is moderated by one's *risk attitude* (i.e., individual difference characteristic in risk tolerance).

Similarly, Sitkin & Weingart (1995) posited that risk perception is mediated by *risk propensity*, which they define as an individual difference characteristic in level of risk tolerance that can be modified and changed through experience. Blais and Weber (2006) attributed differences in risk taking behavior across different domains to differences in perceived risk rather than to differences in risk attitude. The importance of distinguishing between risk perception and risk attitude/risk propensity is highlighted by Cooper et al. (1988), who found that entrepreneurs were more optimistic in their risk perception than were managers but that the two groups did not differ in terms of their risk preferences. These results are consistent with Brockhaus' (1982) findings that both entrepreneurs and managers exhibited a preference for tasks that had moderate levels of risk.

The preceding literature review suggests that "perceived risk" is a multidimensional psychologically-based construct whose elements reflect some aspects of traditional conceptualizations of risk as a statistical property but contains other elements that cannot be represented by objectively derived statistical measures. Indeed, the evidence suggests that "objective" risk often exists independently of its subjective evaluation as "perceived" risk (e.g., Conchar et. al., 2004; Slovic et al., 1986; Mitchell, 1999). Behavioral responses to risky prospects also follow from assessments that are derived from evaluations of "riskiness" in terms of the potential controllability and management of risk (whether real or imagined) geared toward risk reduction, and from more global affective evaluations (dread, catastrophic potential, level of discomfort with uncertainty, etc.) that transcend traditional tenets of "rationality." Moreover, risk perception is not a stable construct but one that varies across individuals, contexts, and cultures. Having outlined some of the variables that define perceived risk, we next turn our attention to methods by which it has been modeled in the literature.

II. The Literature on Modeling Perceived Risk

Most early models of perceived risk have generally attempted to decompose it into its more basic components, and were focused primarily on aspects of uncertainty of choice consequences (including loss potential, potential for negative consequences) and choice importance (e.g., Bettman, 1973; Cunningham, 1967; Horton, 1976; Kogan & Wallach, 1964; Lanzetta & Driscoll, 1968), or were based on more traditional economic considerations in terms of minimizing risk or maximizing return (e.g., Levy & Markowitz, 1979; Peter & Tarpey, 1975). In contrast, Coombs (1975) conceptualized choice behavior in terms of trade-offs between perceived risks and perceived returns among risky prospects. He theorized that people have a non-zero risk tolerance threshold, and that they will prefer options that come closest to their threshold rather than always acting rationally by seeking options that minimize risk in accordance with classical economic theory.

Following Coombs' line of reasoning, Luce (1980) proposed several axiomatic models of financial risk perception that culminated in the Conjoint Expected Risk (CER) model (Luce & Weber, 1986). According to the CER, perceived risk is a linear weighted combination of the probability of zero gain/loss (i.e., of breaking even), the probability of a gain, the probability of a loss, the conditional expectation of a gain, and the conditional expectation of a loss. The conditional expectancies are each raised to unique non-zero exponential coefficients in order to capture individual differences in risk perception. Subsequent research on the CER using the standard lottery paradigm indicated that the power parameters were often close to unity, thus allowing for a simpler specification of the CER model (e.g., Holtgrave & Weber, 1993; Weber, 1988). Notice that the CER models perceived risk within a risk-return framework in which the decision maker considers both gains and losses (as well as their conditional expectancies) when assessing the riskiness of prospects. Although more complex than many of its predecessors, the CER maintains consistency with earlier models in terms of uncertainty (characterized as probability) and importance of consequences (which is implied by the conditional expectancy terms that carry a "harm" or "benefit" interpretation regarding one's financial status quo).

An alternate to the axiomatic approach taken by Luce (1980; Luce & Weber, 1986) in modeling perceived risk in the financial domain is the psychometric approach taken by Slovic and colleagues (Slovic, 1987; Slovic et al., 1986) to model perceived risk in the health and technological domains. Their approach consisted of using psychophysical scaling and multivariate analysis techniques to produce quantitative risk perception representations. Although both models were well-supported by empirical findings within their intended domains, subsequent research examined whether the two approaches could be combined to model perceived risk across domains. The earliest attempt was taken by Holtgrave and Weber (1993), who were interested in determining whether the CER model, the Slovic and colleague's Psychological Risk Dimension model (hereinafter referred to as the PRD model), or a hybrid CER-PRD model would best capture people's risk perceptions in both the financial and health domains. Both the CER model and the PRD model characterize perceived risk as a linear combination of variables. As mentioned above, the CER model represents perceived financial risk as a (weighted) linear combination of 5 variables representing uncertainty over outcomes and conditional expectancies for gains/losses. As such, the CER model represents the more rational, rule-based components of perceived risk developed in the axiomatic measurement tradition (see Weber, 2001 for a review). The PDR model characterizes perceived health/technological risk as a linear function of seven psychological risk dimensions (voluntariness, dread, control, knowledge, catastrophic potential, novelty, equity) developed using a psychometric paradigm. In contrast to the CER model, the PRD model encompasses a more affective set of perceived risk components.

Holtgrave & Weber (1993) tested three models on data in which participants were asked to rate a combined list of financial risks (e.g., investing 20% of savings in a blue-chip stock, investing in one ounce of a precious metal) and health risks (e.g., riding a bicycle 1 mile daily in an urban area, living near a nuclear power plant) on the 5 CER dimensions and the 7 PRD dimensions. Holtgrave and Weber's (1993) results indicated that a hybrid risk perception model that incorporates both objective risk variables (outcomes and related probabilities/expectancies) and more affectively-laden variables (in particular, dread) provided the best fit for risk perception in both the financial and health domains. Their model parameters were estimated using multiple regression analysis, with best fitting model exhibiting the largest R^2 value.

Holtgrave and Weber (1993) were the first to show that perceived risk consisted of both objective information as well as an emotional component. Their findings are also in line with subsequent research documenting that risk perception is influenced as much or more so by affect as by rule-based processing (Loewenstein et al., 2001; Mellers et al., 1997).

In more recent research, Koonce, McAnally, and Mercer (2005) examined how financial statements containing mandatory disclosures about risks and uncertainties impact the risk perception among potential investors (a sample of MBA graduate students). The authors developed and tested a model that combines EU-based variables (probabilities and outcomes) with Slovic et al.'s (1986) psychological risk dimensions. Their results show direct effects of loss outcome information on perceived risk judgments, and further indicated that the psychological risk dimension variables explained a significant amount of variance in risk perception over-and-above what is accounted for by traditional risk variables. This finding was replicated and extended to a more "context rich" disclosure scenario, and showed that disclosure of loss information had both direct and indirect effects on perceived risk. Analysis with structural equation modeling indicated that the indirect effect of loss information occurred through the psychological risk dimension "dread" from the PRD.

As noted previously, it is also important to consider individual differences in risk attitude when modeling perceived risk. In accounting for domain differences in preference for engaging in a risky behavior (e.g., investing 10% of income in government bonds, not wearing sunscreen, telling a friend that his/her significant other made a pass at you, etc.), Weber et al. (2002) decomposed preference into two components: Perceived risk and attitude toward risk. This decomposition provides for different ways in which a particular outcome domain (e.g., financial, health and safety, social, etc.) can influence choice preference through two different but not mutually-exclusive processes: (1) evaluating perceived risk for choice alternatives (i.e., trade-offs on perceived benefits vs. perceived harms), and (2) assessing one's preference for the risk involved with each choice alternative (an individual differences characteristic in one's general positive or negative attitude toward risk). Multiple regression analysis indicated that differences in perceived risk led to inconsistent risk-taking vs. risk-averse preferences, while tended to remain stable across domains. These findings were later replicated by Blais and Weber (2006) using a more sophisticated multi-level modeling approach to isolate the influence of individual differences in risk perception on risk taking behavior.

Regardless of the measurement model used to operationalize perceived risk (axiomatic as in Luce's 1980 and Luce & Weber's 1986 work, or based on psychometric techniques as in Slovic et al.'s, 1986 work), researchers have generally taken a regression approach to decomposing perceived risk into its more basic components. For example, Bettman (1973) specified a series of regression models based on decomposing perceived risk into components related to inherent risk (uncertainty over whether a consumer can make a satisfactory brand choice within a given product class) and handled risk (degree to which inherent uncertainty can be reduced through the amount and usability of information about brands in a given product class). He found that additive regression models explained more variability in perceived risk than did multiplicative models, in line with other contemporary findings supporting a linear modeling approach (e.g., Horton, 1976; Lansetta & Driscoll, 1968; Peter & Tarpey, 1975). Later researchers continued to decompose the elements of perceived risk using the general linear modeling approach in the form of multiple regression, multi-level modeling, or structural equation modeling (e.g., Holtgrave & Weber, 1993; Koonce et al., 2005; Weber et al., 2002).

This review of modeling perceived risk leads to the conclusion that perceived risk can be characterized as a linear combination of variables. As such, the modeling approach used in the literature has been based on some aspect of the general linear model (e.g., multiple regression), or more sophisticated but related linear combination models (multi-level modeling, structural equation modeling). Such models allow researchers to estimate the relative contributions of different theoretic variables in explaining perceived risk. Moreover, individual differences in risk perception, which are important to explaining why the same person may exhibit risk averse behavior in one domain but appear to be risk seeking in another domain (Blais & Weber, 2006; Weber et al., 2002), or for examining differences in risk perception between entrepreneurs and managers (Cooper et al., 1988), can be easily incorporated into models within these statistical frameworks.

The next section first provides the operational definition of the constructs in the proposed theoretic behavioral risk model derived from the informed vantage point provided by our preceding literature review.

A. *Application- Using Financial Decision Making at its Most Basic Level: The Decision to Enter a Business Venture*[1]

The theoretic behavioral finance risk model that is the basis of the present work can be stated as follows:

$$TPR = RR \pm BR \qquad (1)$$

[1] This section is mainly built and further expanded upon R. Yazdipour (2011).

TPR represents the Total Perceived Risk in any given business venture. RR is Resident Risk and represents an objective estimate of risk inherent in any business transaction, is largely estimable from previous data, and therefore, is mathematically tractable. On the other hand, BR, or Behavioral Risk, is a subjective measure of risk based upon psychological assessments of risk or uncertainties that are unrelated to statistical properties such as considerations of importance, evaluation of consequences, and loss potential/unpleasant outcomes. Other theoretical influences on behavioral risk are the well-known biases in subjective probability assessment notion of psychological discomfort produced by risk (e.g., Kahneman, Slovic & Tversky, 1982), as well as more recent evidence for the influence of Affect (e.g., Slovic, et al's "Affect Heuristic;" Neace et al's (2011)).

The objective of the modeling task here is to decompose TPR into its constituent elements as defined in above; and determine (1) which element is weighed more heavily in risk assessments of entry/seed funding decisions, (2) what the relative contribution is of the set of items used to measure RR and BR to perceptions of the total risks assessed in evaluating a given business opportunity, and (3) what differences between entrepreneurs and venture capitalists might there be in the manner in which RR and BR combine to represent TPR. To achieve these goals, the constructs in the theoretic model must be operationalized and that is the main objective of this writing.

1. A Behavioral Risk Model

The approach that we have taken in further developing the proposed risk model in this section is one of going back to the basics and building an intuitive and practical risk model from ground zero. In the present context, our ground zero is defined by making the most basic economic decision of starting a new business venture by an entrepreneur. Such an approach allows us to get a better handle on the whole decision making process and the related mental and cognitive efforts that go into a single decision by an individual. An individual who is not bounded by any corporate or institutional limitation and her/his main concern is her/his own well-being. This also means such a theoretic construct is free of any form of Agency relation. This is an important distinction because almost all the traditional finance's risk theories and models have been developed with highly complex agents, markets, and institutions in mind. That way, many often unrealistic assumptions must be introduced into any analysis; but worse, we could not focus on and learn from the decision making process at its most critical level- the level of an individual. And let's not forget that ALL *final* decisions at *any* corporate or institutional level are in fact *made by one individual.* The behavioral finance literature has recognized such a reality – eg Group Think – in order to arrive at more rigorous models and theories.

With this brief background in mind, we now continue with our risk modeling efforts in this section.

2. Perception Asymmetry

We introduce the Perception Asymmetry as a counterpart to standard finance theory's Information Asymmetry as described in below. But before defining and further discussing the proposed phenomenon, it would be helpful if we first refresh our memory regarding the Prospect Theory and the Affect Heuristic.

According to Prospect Theory (PT), there are two distinct phases to each decision- an initial phase called Editing or Framing; and a second phase called Evaluation phase. The editing phase includes a number of operations that simplify decision problems before they are sent for evaluation. Options are evaluated via the Value Function so that a final decision can be made regarding the decision problems under consideration.

According to Affect theory, subjective impressions of "goodness" or "badness" can act as a heuristic, capable of producing fast perceptual judgments. For example, stocks perceived as "good" are judged to have *low* risks and *high* returns and stocks perceived as "bad" are judged to have *low* returns and *high* risks.

By building upon the Prospect Theory and the Affect heuristic as just mentioned, and using our example of entrepreneurs and venture capitalists for illustration, we propose that the perceptions of both entrepreneurs and venture capitalists, and consequently their judgments, will be shaped by the triple effects of:

1. The Prospect Theory's editing operations which include Coding, Combination, Segregation, and Cancellation,
2. The Prospect Theory's value function where "probability weights" are assigned, and
3. The Affect heuristic's capability of producing perceptual judgments.

In addition to above, the working of the brain would add the fourth effect; but for now we will limit our coverage to the key psychological phenomena[2].

We now define Perception Asymmetry as the situation under which a perception gap exists for at least one party to a transaction. More specifically, in case of our present discussion, we define Perception Asymmetry (PA) as the situation under which a perception gap exists between an entrepreneur and a venture capitalist (VC) regarding the same business opportunity, its gain and loss potentials, and consequently the opportunity's perceived value. Furthermore, the only situation in which such a gap will not exist is when both the entrepreneur and the VC in question share the same psyche; something that is not physically possible.

We suspect the proposed imbalance would help create a better understanding for both parties regarding each other's views on a transaction like a seed funding deal. Such an understanding may minimize the perception asymmetry and consequently bring the parties closer to a mutually beneficial decision and ultimately conclusion of a deal.

III. Resident Risks and Behavioral Risks: Toward a Behavioral Finance Risk Model

Some behavioral finance scholars, especially Slovic and Olsen, have advocated that risk is not "something out there". By that, they mean risk is not an evidence-based phenomenon like standard deviation, beta, or other variations thereof that can be measured and used in financial decision making[3]. Put differently, risk does not exist "out there" so that we a) observe it, b) measure and analyze it, and c) use it as an input in our Expected Utility (EU)-based calculations. Slovic (1987) attributes business risk to individual survival risk where he says, "Humans have an additional capability that allows them to alter their environment as well as respond to it. This capacity both

---

[2] We are not specifically discussing other heuristics and biases for two main reasons. First, the Prospect Theory and Affect cover most, if not all, of such heuristics and biases. Second, given this is a preliminary framework, we'd rather to stay on the central issues to prevent any confusion.

[3] Needless to say that the standard finance theory definitions of risk have no relevance at all to a great majority of entrepreneurial finance problems where there is little or no historical data "out there" to be measured in the first place! For example, in case of startups almost all the data are projected data and are contained in a highly guarded Business Plan.

creates and reduces risk"[4]. He further adds that the "concept risk means different things to different people"[5]. Moreover, as we will see in this chapter, affect plays one of the most important roles in the perception of risk by individuals[6]. For example if a person has a positive affect regarding a given venture, she/he may perceive the risk in that venture much less than the risks perceived by other individuals with a lower level of affect for the same exact venture under otherwise the same exact circumstances.

Olsen specifically states that, "all risk that is acted upon must be perceived risk because perception is based upon sensory data. We can only sense the 'real world' because we have no other way of being informed."[7] This effectively means risk is a phenomenon that is created in our psyche- the "in here" risk versus the "out there risk" phrase that we use in this chapter.

However, and especially from a more applied point of view, we argue that risks and uncertainties are not completely perceived "in here" either (in our psyche). This can be seen clearly when we break down the notion of total risk and uncertainty into its components and discuss "Resident Risks" below. We then believe the truth about the sources of risks probably lie somewhere between "out there" and "in here". To get our discussion started, we define risk and uncertainty as follows.

Total (Perceived) Risk and Uncertainty = "Resident Risks" + or – "Behavioral Risks"

A. *Resident Risk: Risk as the "Other Side of a Business Opportunity Coin"*

First note that due to the nature of the topic, we use the terms risk and uncertainty interchangeably throughout this writing. Second, for simplicity and illustration we use the decision to launch a business venture, a business opportunity, as an example. Now think of "Resident Risks" as the type of risks that actually *reside* in, or are native to, a given business opportunity; without which the opportunity would be

---

[4] Slovic, Paul, Science, Vol 236, 1987, p 280. Emphasis is ours.

[5] Ibid, p 283

[6] According to Olsen (2011), culture, including trust, is another source of risk. However, in this writing we will limit our discussions to the factors stated in above.

[7] See chapter 4, Olsen.

riskless. (Riskless in the sense of a short-term U.S. Treasury Bill.) In other words, in our example, risk is the "other side of a *business opportunity coin*'. That is, such risk gets created when an individual enters a venture; a business opportunity.

We especially use the coin analogy to make the point that Resident Risk (RR) automatically comes with any selected and implemented business opportunity; just like throwing a coin that comes with it known odds of success/fail. Of course, measuring success/failure rates in business are much more complicated; but still doable. Another analogy for the definition is water and the wetness of water. That is, one cannot exist without the other; and you know if you throw yourself in the water, you will get wet, and the odds are 100% in your favor! Just like tossing a coin with well-defined outcomes, we can also define the possible outcomes in a launch decision. For example, success can mean reaching $5M sales in three years and failure can mean not reaching that sales threshold by the third year.

Additionally, dissecting Total Perceived Risk as such has another theoretical and empirical advantage. It allows us to have a significant portion of the total risk measurable and concentrate on its elusive component- the behavioral risk component.

B. Determinants of Resident Risk

In anticipation of making the resident risk component operational and consequently measurable, we can proceed as follows. Imagine yourself as an entrepreneur who has not only found a unique business opportunity, but has also developed a non-working prototype of her product and wants to launch the business by first perfecting the prototype and then mass producing and selling the finished product. She also needs capital to do all the above. You may also imagine yourself at the other side of the transaction and as a venture capitalist who is considering funding such an entrepreneur. Given this background, we can list and define the following factors as the key determinants of residual risk.

a. Commercialization and Technology risk factor- the risk of taking an opportunity or a prototype and turning it into a fully functional product or service that consumers will pay to use it,
b. Market risk factor - whether or not a profitable and sustainable market will emerge for the envisioned product/service,

c. Management risk factor - whether or not the entrepreneur behind the opportunity and her team will succeed in executing the envisioned business strategies
d. Financing risk factor - whether or not the entrepreneur and her team can raise the needed capital on a timely basis to execute the envisioned business strategies, and finally,
e. Macro risk factors- including regulatory risks, environmental risks, etc.

The above risks certainly exit "out there" in and around *any* business opportunity. However, they do *not* exist in vacuum as there must be a real asset in the physical world to contain such native risks. And that is exactly why we refer collectively to these risks as Resident Risks.[8]

C. Behavioral Risks

The "Behavioral Risk" component is mainly shaped by the editing, evaluating, and affect processes as described earlier in this chapter. As shown by the risk equation, behavioral risks can either increase or decrease the total risk. The increase part seems very intuitive by the standards of the traditional finance; although that is not the case for the decrease part as it can easily be ignored as a behavioral "anomaly"! To a behavioral economist however, the decrease is a result of the affect heuristic.

Furthermore, according to the proposed risk framework and the theories behind it – Prospect Theory and Affect Heuristic – the behavioral risk portion of the total risk is our own creation. In other words, when we consider a set of opportunities for evaluation and final selection, we automatically, and possibly unknowingly, *construct* a portion of the risks that involve all those opportunities. Given the current state of brain technology, this is the type of risk that is very hard, if not impossible, to quantify.

---

[8] Resident Risks can become *the only* risks, and therefore the only *"real" risks*, if we take all the heuristics out of the simple equation suggested in this section. In such a case, Total Risk is equivalent to the Total Risk under standard finance paradigm, and measurable. But again, to take the behavioral risk component out is equivalent to assuming a "mind of God" for a normal earth-bound human being.

D. Behavioral Risk Processes

Although discussion on making the behavioral risk component operational is well above and beyond the present writing; however we can still list and describe the four underlying processes that produce it as follows.

a. Framing processes
b. Evaluation processes
c. Affective processes, and
d. Other non-Affect processes like Overconfidence, Availability, Anchoring, etc.

All the above processes are as described in this chapter.

IV. Operationalizing the Proposed Behavioral Finance Risk Model

A. A Literature Review on Operationalizing Perceived Risk in General

Although many operational definitions of perceived risk have been used in the extent literature depending upon the content and context of a decision situation (e.g., Conchar et. al., 2004, Mitchell, 1999), the most common manner of soliciting peoples' opinions of risk has been through rating perceptions of the "riskiness" of a given choice set or behavior. Some of the more representative examples of measuring perceived risk in the finance, economic, and psychological literatures are shown in Table 1.

Table 1. ***Some representative operational definitions of perceived risk from the finance, economics, and psychology literatures.***

Article	Operational Definition of Perceived Risk
Bettman (1973)	Ratings for each item (typical grocery products) on a scale (-8 to +8) in a paired-comparison procedure asking which item in the pair would be more risky to shop for in an imaginary store (no brand names used) or their usual store (with brand labels on products).
Peter & Tarpey (1975)	7-point semantic differential scales on rating loss probability (automobile purchase preference) of 6 risk facets.

Holtgrave & Weber (1993)	rated overall riskiness of activities (health, financial) on a 1 to 100 scale.
Sitkin & Weingart (1995)	Four 7-point scales asking participants to rate characteristics of a given scenario with anchors "significant opportunity"/"significant threat"; loss potential/gain potential; positive/negative; and success likelihood with anchors very unlikely/very likely.
Weber & Milliman (1997)	"gut level" assessment of how risky X is (in 5 relevant domains) on a 5-point scale with anchors of "not at all risky" to "extremely risky."
Ganzach (2000)	"how risky" X is on a 9-point scale with anchors of very low and very high (where X is one of 30 international stock portfolios).
Weber et al. (2002); Blais & Weber (2006)	ratings on a scale of 500 to 600 for how risky each given choice was (used pairs of lotteries differing in expected gains/losses).
Koonce et al. (2005)	Overall, how risky is [particular financial item being rated] to the company on a 0 (no risk) to 100 (high risk) scale.
Ferguson & Gallagher (2007)	Two 7point scales assessing personal outcome effectiveness ("how effective do you think" with anchors of not very to very effective) and procedural risk ("how risky do you perceive" with anchors not at all to very risky) for a health behavior (flu shot).
Ganzach et al. (2008)	"how risky" X is on a 7-point scale with anchors of low risk, high risk (8 "investment" prospects)

Of primary importance in developing models of risk perception is to obtain a valid and reliable measure of it. To that end, Gonzach et al. (2008) assessed the construct validity of risk perception measures and concluded that single-item measures more accurately captured the construct of "risk perception" than did multiple-item measures, which tend to confound risk perception with related concepts (such as the attractiveness of a prospect or with expected return). Other research also disentangles the concepts of risk perception from judgments of attractiveness indicating that they are two distinct psychological constructions (Weber et al., 1992). As mentioned earlier, it is also important to measure risk perception without confounding it with risk attitude/propensity (e.g., Sitkin & Weingart, 1995; Weber et al., 2002; Blais & Weber,

2006). Thus, based on these psychometric findings, we adopt a single-item measure of *Total Perceived Risk* for purposes of operationalizing the main construct of our behavioral risk model, an example of which appears in Table 2 at the end of this section. The following discussion moves toward the operational definition of the other two constructs of which Total Perceived Risk is theorized to be composed, *Resident Risk* and *Behavioral Risk.*

Resident risk captures the more traditional decision theoretic components of risk, such as outcomes and their associated probabilities, or outcome variance over a probability distribution. It is an "objective" component of Total Perceived Risk, and is readily operationalized as a probability of success/failure for a given business venture, or as the variability of successes/failures over an entire class of similar business ventures from pre-existing data sources. Probabilities (whether considered alone or in combination with outcomes to form expectancies) are common to many models of perceived risk (Bettman, 1973; Cunningham, 1967; Kogan & Wallach, 1964; Peter & Ryan, 1976; Peter & Tarpey, 1975; Stone & Winter, 1987; Ganzach, 2000; Ganzach et al., 2008; Luce, 1980, Luce & Weber, 1986; Holtgrave & Weber, 1993; Koonce et al., 2005). As such, Resident Risk is deemed an important theoretical aspect of perceived risk though it does not completely define it.

Aside from considerations of objective risk measures are those that tap into the more subjective, psychologically-grounded measures of risk, which we have chosen to label "Behavioral Risk." Scholars of perceived risk recognized the need to incorporate non-statistical risk measures in their theories due to the general dissatisfaction with Expected Utility models and their variants in adequately capturing choice behavior (e.g., Kahneman & Tversky, 1979; Schoemaker, 1982; Luce, 2003; Weber, 1994). Behavioral risk can be further partitioned into its more basic components derived from our earlier review of the literature. These components represent aspects of a given business venture, such as importance of entering into/providing funding for a given business opportunity, the potential (perceived) gain/loss associated with entry/funding decisions, and the potential for adverse or negative consequences associated with entry/funding decisions. Each of these aspects can be measured on 100-point scales with appropriate anchors for low and high levels of the construct being assessed (e.g., for importance of entering into X business venture, 1 = not at all important and 100 = extremely important. See Table 2 for other examples). In addition to these common elements of perceived risk, we add Affective variables, such as those provided by Slovic and colleagues (Slovic, 1987; Slovic et al., 1986; Slovic et al., 2002), and a psychological discomfort variable (Neace et al., in press) representing the degree to which uncertainty in a business venture impacts the decision maker's level of comfort with risk. Lastly, we propose that behavioral risk assessments are, in part, separable from one's general risk attitude (Blais & Weber, 2006; Cho & Lee, 2006; Sitkin & Weingart, 1995; Weber et al., 2002), and include a measure of risk attitude under the Behavioral Risk category in order to capture individual differences in risk tolerance.

Table 2 that follows presents examples of items and their operational definitions for constructs in our theoretical Behavioral Finance Risk Model. The variables are categorized broadly as those related to Resident Risk, and those related to Behavioral Risk. Under the *Resident Risk* category are objective probability estimates for success/failure for a particular business venture within a given industry. Such data are available from leading market and business industry sources. In addition, estimates of variability in business venture success within a given industry can be derived from the same objective data.

The Behavioral Risk category is composed of the following measures in the order that they appear in Column 1 of Table 2: Importance (adapted from Bettman, 1973), the Conjoint Expected Risk or CER model variables (adapted from Luce & Weber, 1986), which include measures of uncertainty over outcomes (maintaining the status quo, potential for gain, potential for loss), and conditional expectancies related to gains and losses. In addition, the Behavioral Risk category contains the 7 variables from the Psychological Risk Dimension or PRD model (adapted from Koonce et al., 2005) that capture a more global and affective evaluation of a given business opportunity, which are, in part, related to the affect heuristic (Slovic et al., 2002). Also included under Behavioral Risk is a measure of psychological discomfort to capture the degree to which uncertainty regarding a business opportunity creates a state of increased physiological arousal that is experienced as unpleasant (as theorized by Neace et al., in press, and for which empirical evidence has recently been obtained by Neace et al., 2010).

Finally, in order to separate the influence of individual differences in risk perception from one's overall risk attitude (viz. Weber et al., 2002), we include a risk attitude variable in our operational behavioral risk model.

Table 2. ***Examples of measurement items to assess the Total Perceived Risk, Resident Risk, and Behavioral Risk constructs of the proposed Behavioral Finance Risk Model.***

Construct	Operational Definition of Construct
Total Perceived Risk	Overall, how risky is [entering into/providing funding for] X business opportunity? 1 = not at all risky, 100 = extremely risky
Resident Risk	
Probability	Various success probabilities associated with business ventures across different industries, measured from objective sources. An intuitive data source would be historical data from the venture capital industry regarding success/failure statistics for say new ventures in a given industry. Such data also contains profile of entrepreneurs that further help the testing process.
Variability	Various success/failure rates associated with business ventures across different industries, measured from objective sources just like above. Actual variance estimates from data.
Behavioral Risk	
Importance of ROI	How important is achieving a satisfactory return on your investment to your [decision to enter/provide funding for X business opportunity]? 1 = not at all important, 100 = extremely important
Importance of investment	How much of an investment are you willing to make (in terms of time, money, other resources) in deciding to [enter/provide funding] for X business opportunity? 1 = very little, 100 = very much
Potential to maintain the status quo	What do you think your chances are of breaking even if you decide [to enter/provide funding] for X business opportunity? 1 = very unlikely, 100 = extremely likely
Potential for positive outcome	What do you think your chances are of getting a positive return on your investment if you decide [to enter/provide funding] for X business opportunity? 1 = very unlikely, 100 = extremely likely
Potential for	What do you think your chances are of experiencing a loss on

negative outcome	your investment if you decide [to enter/provide funding] for X business opportunity? 1 = very unlikely, 100 = extremely likely
Conditional expectation of a positive outcome	Suppose your decision to [enter/provide seed funding for] results in an overall gain to investors. How large a gain would you expect in this situation? 1 = very small, 100 = very large
Conditional expectation of a negative outcome	Suppose your decision to [enter/provide seed funding for] results in an overall loss to investors. How large a loss would you expect in this situation? 1 = very small, 100 = very large
Voluntariness	How likely is it that you would voluntarily decide to [enter/provide seed funding for] X business opportunity without knowing the level or risk involved? 1 = involuntary, 100 = completely voluntary
Dread	How likely is it that you would dread (feel fear, or worry excessively) about the potential for negative consequences from your decision to [enter/provide seed funding for] X business opportunity? 1 = very unlikely, 100 = extremely likely
Control	How much do you believe your skill and diligence allow you to have control over potentially negative consequences of your decision to [enter/provide seed funding for] X business opportunity? 1 = very difficult to control, 100 = very easy to control
Knowledge	How knowledgeable are you about the precise risks associated with your decision to [enter/provide seed funding] for X business opportunity? 1 = not at all knowledgeable, 100 = extremely knowledgeable
Catastrophic potential	How likely is it that your decision to [enter/provide seed funding for] X business opportunity will end in a worse-case financial disaster? 1 = very unlikely, 100 = extremely likely
Novelty	How much do you believe the risks associated in your decision to [enter/provide seed funding for] X business opportunity are ones that are unfamiliar to you, as opposed to risks that you are familiar with? 1 = very unfamiliar, 100 = very familiar
Equity	How likely do you think it is that any outcomes (good or bad) from your decision to [enter/provide seed funding for] X business opportunity will be fairly distributed? 1 = very unlikely, 100 = extremely likely

Psychological Discomfort	Derived measure from SAM affect and SAM arousal scales, producing a scale of 1 to 18, with higher values indicating more psychological discomfort. Details in Neace et al., 2010.
Risk Attitude	In general, what is your attitude toward taking risks such as [entering/investing in] new business opportunities? 1 = not at all positive about taking business risks, 100 = very positive about taking business risks

B. Empirical Test of the Proposed Behavioral Finance Risk Model

1. Background

Before we discuss the empirical model proposed in this writing, what follows provides a rather brief background on our efforts in such regard.

First, Yazdipour (2011) suggested Lewis' "Principal Principle" – which is a theory linking credence (belief in evidence) to chance (the probabilistic nature of the evidence) – as a possible candidate for testing the Behavioral Risk Model as discussed in the present writing. However, we learned that after a thorough discussion of some common mistakes associated with using the "Principal Principle", Meacham (2010) had presented a methodology that was robust to the errors of previous "Principal Principle" presentations. While interesting and rigorous, the "Principal Principle" is more in line with Bayesian belief updating than it is in capturing the nature of the behavioral risk model as proposed above.

Second, alternate operationalization is also available from recent work by Hsee and Rottenstreich (2004, see also Rottenstreich & Hsee, 2001), who examined the role of affect in risk perception, coupled with the hypothesized behavior of individuals as outlined in Yazdipour (2011, p. 20) and that we paraphrase below (please note the decision to enter any venture can only be signified by committing the needed investment or funds and that is why we use entry and funding interchangeable at times) :

1. Final entry/funding decisions are based on perceived gains and losses (relative to an initial reference point W = initial wealth state) stemming from an

evaluation of the value for each given business opportunity in a set of such business opportunities;

2. The level of "comfort" about the perceived risks inherent in each business opportunity under consideration.

Such judgments and decisions are theorized to be shaped by prospect theory's editing functions (coding, combination, segregation, and cancellation), prospect theory's value function (particularly the subjective weight given to probabilities of success/failure and how they are assigned), and affective theories which address the issue of perceptual judgments.

The Proposed Testing Model

Given above, what follows then is an operationalization of the conceptual model suggested in Equation 1 based upon consideration of the various factors that influence perceived risk. Specifically,

$$R = V^{(1-\alpha)} A^{\alpha} C \qquad (2)$$

Reading Equation 2 from left to right, R is the Total (Perceived) Risk in any given business opportunity, V is the value function from prospect theory (Kahneman & Tversky, 1979), A is an Affective intensity parameter, C is a Comfort (or homeostasis) parameter, and α is an Affective focus coefficient bounded by 0 and 1.

V captures the perceived value of a given choice in business opportunities based upon a behavioral assessment of their resident risk (through its decision weight parameter, π), and is therefore sensitive to well-established cognitive biases (such as framing effects, overconfidence, etc.). The *V* parameter models decision weights in the valuation of a choice in business opportunities as a function of different levels of probabilities, *p*:

$V = \pi(p)v(x) + \pi(1 - p)v(y)$, where *p* is taken as a measure of Resident Risk in Equation 1 and as defined early on in this work.

A captures the hypothesized Affective component associated with a choice in a set of business opportunities. This parameter of the model captures affective elements of the decision process, and is therefore sensitive to effects influenced by such elements as how the decision maker "feels" about each business opportunity, and how such feelings influence perceived riskiness, as posited by the Affect Heuristic and other affective theories.

C captures the decision maker's level of comfort with the perceived risks for a given set of business opportunities, which models the associated uncertainty-induced psychological discomfort from Neace (2010). *C* is assumed to vary from individual to individual, and can be used to model individual differences in thresholds for how much discomfort can be tolerated for a given choice (i.e., homeostasis) as posited by Konopka and Ackerly (2011).

Finally, α provides a measure of the extent to which a decision maker is focusing on affective or cognitive components associated with a given choice among business opportunities. It is bounded by 0 (no focus on affective element) and 1 (complete focus on affect at the expense of cognitive processing).

Model's Predictions

The model in Equation 2 is able to make some predictions that are in line with the hypotheses about the behavior of both entrepreneurs and venture capitalists presented by Yazdipour (2011). In particular, consider the model's predictions at the extremes of the affective focus coefficient, α:

When $\alpha = 0$, R = VC. Here, the model predicts that the risk assessed for a given business opportunity is a function of V from prospect theory weighted by the degree of comfort the decision maker has with uncertainty or risk inherent in the venture. This model might well reflect the fact that venture capitalists are mostly concerned with evaluating the Resident Risks in choosing whether to provide seed funding for a particular business opportunity, as well as their individual level of comfort with such uncertainty.

At the other extreme, when $\alpha = 1$, R = AC, reflecting that the risk assessed for a given business opportunity is a function of Affective intensity of the venture, weighted by the degree of Comfort the decision maker has with its associated risk. This model might well reflect that entrepreneurs are more passionate in their assessments of risk associated with a given business venture, focusing more on the Affective than the cognitive aspects of the situation. As such, their choice of which business opportunity to pursue is less affected by cognitive (or "rational") assessment of resident risk and more in line with their affective assessment of the potential for success.

In between these two extremes, the model predicts that total perceived risk varies as a function of value (which is based upon an assessment of resident risks), affect, and the degree to which the decision maker is focus of the affective components over more careful cognitive assessments of a set of business opportunities. Moreover, the model proposes that perceived risk is, in part, a function of how comfortable the decision maker is about one business venture compared to other such opportunities. Thus, the model yields testable predictions about the differences in the assessment of Resident Risk vs. emotional aspects between entrepreneurs and venture capitalists, as hypothesized by Yazdipour (2011).

The model may also help to close the "perceptual gap" that is hypothesized to exist between entrepreneurs and venture capitalists (the *perceptual asymmetry* introduced by Yazdipour, 2011, p 16) by examining differences in an opportunity's perceived value as a function of resident risk (probability of success/failure), affect, and individual thresholds for how much discomfort for uncertainty/risk can be tolerated between entrepreneurs and venture capitalists who are evaluating the same business opportunity.

In general, the model's prediction begins with a baseline established by prospect theory, and suggests that the concavity or convexity of the S-shaped value function will become more or less extreme due to adding parameters for affective intensity and degree of comfort. The model's predictions can be tested against a purely rational model (given by classical expected value theory), as well as against predictions made by prospect theory (that is, in the absence of considerations for affect and comfort-levels for risk).

V. Conclusion and Summary

The testable Behavioral Finance Risk Model as advanced in Equation 2 builds upon the Prospect Theory via parameter V, by considering how Affect influences perceived risk via parameter A, and by incorporating the need for the decision maker to reach a manageable level of Comfort with the involved uncertainties via parameter C. Additionally, the model's three variables can be readily operationalized as discussed in the present work. The techniques used to model value (V) from various tests of prospect theory can be used to operationalize that component of the proposed model. Affect parameter, A, can be measured using operational definitions from tests of the Affect Heuristic, and the Comfort parameter, C, has an operational definition derived from recent empirical research and mentioned in this work. The Affective intensity parameter, α, is a free parameter that can be estimated from data.

Regarding the nature and type of actual data, the venture capital industry in the USA is the prime source for collecting the needed data for testing the model proposed in the present work. Some suggestions were made in the paper in this regard.

REFERENCES

Baird, I. S., & Thomas, H. (1985). Toward a contingency model of strategic risk taking. *Academy of Management Review, 10*, 230–243.

Bargh, J. A. (1997). The automaticity of everyday life. In R. S. Wyer, Jr. (Ed.), *The automaticity of everyday life: Advances in social cognition, vol. 10*. Mahwah, NJ: Erlbaum.

Bauer, R. A. (1967). Consumer behavior as risk taking. In D. F. Cox (Ed.), *Risk taking and information handling in consumer behavior*, Boston, MA: Graduate School of Business Administration, Harvard University.

Bechara, A., Tranel, D., & Damasio, A. R. (2000). Poor judgment in spite of high intellect: Neurological evidence for emotional intelligence. In R. Bar-On, and J. D. Parker (Eds.), *The handbook of emotional intelligence: Theory, development, assessment, and application at home, school, and in the workplace* (pp. 192–214). San Francisco, CA: Jossey-Bass.

Bettman, J. R. (1973). Perceived risk and its components: A model and empirical test. *Journal of Marketing Research, 10*, 184–190.

Blais, A-R., & Weber, E. U. (2006). A domain-specific risk-taking (DOSBERT) scale for adult populations. *Judgment and Decision Making, 1*, 33–47.

Bontempo, R. N., Bottom, W. P., & Weber, E. U. (1997). Cross-cultural differences in risk perception: A model-based approach. *Risk Analysis, 17*, 479–488.

Brockhaus, R. H. (1982). The psychology of the entrepreneur. In C. A. Kent, D. L. Sexton, & K. G. Vesper (Eds.), *The encyclopedia of entrepreneurship*. Englewood Cliffs, NJ: Prentice Hall.

Cho, J., & Lee, J. (2006). An integrated model of risk and risk-reducing strategies. *Journal of Business Research, 59*, 112–120.

Conchar, M. P., Zinkhan, G. M., Peters, C., & Olavarrieta, S. (2004). An integrated framework of the conceptualization of consumers' perceived-risk processing. *Academy of Marketing Science Journal, 32*, 418–436.

Coombs, C. H. (1975). Portfolio theory and the measurement of risk. In M. F. Kaplan, & S. Schwartz (Eds.). *Human judgment and decision*. New York, NY: Academic Press.

Cooper, A. C., Woo, C. Y., & Dunkelberg, W. C. (1988). Entrepreneurs' perceived chances of success. *Journal of Business Venturing, 3*, 97–108.

Cunningham, S. M. (1967). The major dimensions of perceived risk. In D. F. Cox (Ed.), *Risk taking and information handling in consumer behavior*, Boston, MA: Graduate School of Business Administration, Harvard University.

Ferguson, E., & Gallagher, L. (2007). Message framing with respect to decisions about vaccination: The roles of frame valence, frame method, and perceived risk. *British Journal of Psychology, 98*, 667–680.

Finucane, M. L., Alhakami, A., Slovic, P., & Johnson, S. M. (2000). The affect heuristic in judgments of risks and benefits. *Journal of Behavioral Decision Making, 13*, 1–17.

Froot, K., Scharfstein, D., & Stein, J. (1993). Risk management: Coordinating corporate investment and financing policies. *Journal of Finance, 48*, 1629–1658.

Ganzach, Y. (2000). Judging risk and return of financial assets. *Organizational Behavior and Human Decision Processes, 83*, 353–370.

Ganzach, Y., Ellis, S., Pazy, A., & Ricci-Siag, T. (2008). On the perception and operationalization of risk perception. *Judgment and Decision Making, 3*, 317–324.

Hsee, C. K., & Rottenstreich, Y. (2004). Music, pandas, and muggers: On the affective psychology of value. *Journal of Experimental Psychology: General, 133*, 23–30.

Holtgrave, D. R., & Weber, E. U. (1993). Dimensions of risk perception for financial and health risks. *Risk Analysis, 13*, 553–558.

Horton, R. L. (1976). The structure of decision risk: Some further progress. *Journal of the Academy of Marketing Science, 4*, 694–706.

Huber, O., Beutter, C., Montoya, J., & Huber, O. W. (2001). Risk-defusing behavior: Towards an understanding of risky decision making. *European Journal of Cognitive Psychology, 13*, 409–426.

Jacoby, J., & Kaplan, L. (1972). The components of perceived risk. In M. Venkatesan (Ed.), *Proceedings of the 3rd annual conference of the Association for Consumer Research* (pp. 382–393). Chicago, IL: Association of Consumer Research.

Johnson, E. J. (2004). Rediscovering risk. *Journal of Public Policy and Marketing, 23*, 2–6.

Jorgensen, B., & Kirschenheiter, M. (2003). Discretionary risk disclosures. *Accounting Review, 78*, 449–469.

Kahneman, D. (2003) A prospective on judgment and choice. *American Psychologist, 58*, 697–720.

Kahneman, D., Slovic, P., & Tversky, A. (1982). *Judgment under uncertainty: Heuristics and biases.* New York, NY: Cambridge University Press.

Kahneman, D., & Tversky, A. (1979). Prospect theory: An analysis of decision under risk. *Econometrica, 47*, 263–291.

Kogan, N., & Wallach, M. A. (1964). Risk taking: A study in cognition and personality. New York, NY: Holt, Reinhart, & Winston.

Konopka & Ackley (2011) Contributions of Neuroscience to Financial Decision Making– In R. Yazdipour (Ed.), *Advances in Entrepreneurial Finance: With Application from Behavioral Finance and Economics*, Springer.

Koonce, L., McAnally, M. L., & Mercer, M. (2005). How do investors judge the risk of financial items? *Accounting Review, 80*, 221–241.

Lanzetta, J. T., & Driscoll, J. M. (1968). Effects of uncertainty and importance on information search in decision making. *Journal of Personality and Social Psychology, 10*, 479–486.

Ledoux, J. E. (2000). Emotion circuits in the brain. *Annual Review of Neuroscience, 23*, 155–184.

Lipshitz, R., & Strauss, O. (1997). Coping with uncertainty: A naturalistic decision-making analysis. *Organizational Behavior and Human Decision Processes, 69*, 149–163.

Loewenstein, G. F., Weber, E. U., Hsee, C. K., & Welch, N. (2001). Risk as feelings. *Psychological Bulletin, 127*, 267–286.

Luce, R. D. (1980). Several possible measures of risk. *Theory and Decision, 12*, 217–228.

Luce, R. D., & Weber, E. U. (1986). An axiomatic theory of conjoint expected risk. *Journal of Mathematical Psychology, 30*, 188–205.

MacCrimmon, K. R., & Wehrung, D. A. (1990). Characteristics of risk taking executives. *Management Science, 36*, 422–435.

March, J. G., & Shapiro, Z. (1987). Managerial perspectives on risk. *Management Science, 33*, 1404–1418.

Mellers, B. A., Schwartz, A., Ho, K., & Ritov, I. (1997). Decision Affect Theory: Emotional reactions to the outcomes of risky options. *Psychological Science, 8*, 423–429.

Meacham, C. J. G. (2010). Two mistakes regarding the principal principle. *British Journal for the Philosophy of Science, 61*, 407–431.

Mitchell, V-W. (1999). Consumer perceived risk: Conceptualizations and models. *European Journal of Marketing*, 33, 163–195.

Neace, W. P., Deer, K., & Barnard, J. (September, 2010). *The impact of uncertainty-induced psychological discomfort on choice preference: Testing a novel theory of decision making under uncertainty.* Paper presented at the Annual Meeting of the Academy of Behavioral Finance, Chicago, IL.

Neace, W. P., Deer, K., Michaud, S., & Bolling, L. (2011). Uncertainty is psychologically uncomfortable: A proposed theoretic framework for studying judgments and decision-making under uncertainty and risk. In R. Yazdipour (Ed.), *Advances in Entrepreneurial Finance: With Application from Behavioral Finance and Economics*, Springer.

Olsen, R. A. (2011). Financial Risk Perceptions: A Behavioral Perspective. In R. Yazdipour (Ed.), *Advances in Entrepreneurial Finance: With Application from Behavioral Finance and Economics*, Springer.

Peter, J. P., & Ryan, M. J. (1976). An investigation of perceived risk at the brand level. *Journal of Marketing Research, 13*, 184–188.

Peter, J. P., & Tarpey, L. X., Sr. (1975). A comparative analysis of three consumer decision strategies. *Journal of Consumer Research, 2*, 29–37.

Pollatsek, A., & Tversky, A. (1970). A theory of risk. *Journal of Mathematical Psychology, 7*, 540–553.

Roselius, E. (1971). Consumer rankings of risk reduction methods. *Journal of Marketing, 35*, 56–61.

Rottenstreich, Y., & Hsee, C. K. (2001). Money, kisses, and electric shocks: On the affective psychology of risk. *Psychological Science, 12*, 185–190.

Schoemaker, P. J. H. (1982). The expected utility model: It's variants, purposes, evidence and limitations. *Journal of Economic Literature, 20*, 529–563.

Schwarz, N. (2002). Feelings as information: Moods influence judgments and processing
strategies. In T. Golovich, D. Griffin, & D. Kahneman (Eds.), *Heuristics and biases: The psychology of intuitive judgment*, (pp. 534-547). New York, NY: Cambridge University Press.

Sitkin, S. B., & Pablo, A. L. (1992). Reconceptualizing the determinants of risk behavior. *Academy of Management Review, 17*, 9–38.

Sitkin, S. B., & Weingart, L. R. (1995). Determinants of risky decision making behavior: A test of the mediating role of risk perceptions and propensity. *Academy of Management Journal, 38*, 1573–1592.

Slovic, P. (1987). Perceptions of risk. *Science, 236*, 280–285.

Slovic, P., Funucane, M. L., Peters, E., & MacGregor, D. G. (2002). The affect heuristic. In T. Gilovich, D. Griffin, & D. Kahneman (Eds.), *Heuristics and biases: The psychology of intuitive judgment*. New York, NY: Cambridge University Press.

Slovic, P., Finucane, M. L., Peters, E., & MacGregor, D. G. (2004). Risk as analysis and risk as feelings: Some thoughts about affect, reason, risk, and rationality. *Risk Analysis, 24*, 311–322.

Slovic, P., Fischhoff, B., & Lichtenstein, S. (1986). The psychometric study of risk perception. In V. T. Covello, J. Menkes, & J. Mumpower (Eds.), Risk evaluation and management. New York, NY: Plenum Press.

Stone, R. N., & Winter, F. W. (1987). Risk: Is it still uncertainty times consequences? In R. W. Belk and others (Eds.), *Proceedings of the American Marketing Association*. Chicago, IL.

Weber, E. U. (1988). A descriptive measure of risk. *Acta Psychologia, 69*, 185–203.

Weber, E. U. (1994). From subjective probabilities to decision weights: The effect of asymmetric loss functions on the evaluation of uncertain outcomes and events. *Psychological Bulletin, 115*, 228–242.

Weber, E. U. (2001). Decision and choice: Risk, empirical studies. In N. J. Smelser & P. B. Baltes (Eds.), *International encyclopedia of the social and behavioral sciences*. Oxford, UK: Elsevier Science, Ltd.

Weber, E. U., Anderson, C. J., & Birnbaum, M. H. (1992). A theory of perceived risk and attractiveness. *Organizational Behavior and Human Decision Processes, 52*, 492–523.

Weber, E. U., Blais, A-R., & Betz, N. E. (2002). A domain-specific risk-attitude scale: Measureing risk perceptions and risk behaviors. *Journal of Behavioral Decision Making, 15*, 263–290.

Weber, E. U., & Milliman, R. (1997). Perceived risk attitudes: Relating risk perception to risky choice. *Management Science, 43*, 122–143.

Yazdipour, R. (2011). A Behavioral Finance Approach to Decision Making in Entrepreneurial Finance. In R. Yazdipour (Ed.), *Advances in Entrepreneurial Finance: With Application from Behavioral Finance and Economics*, Springer.

Zajonc, R. B. (1998). Emotions. In D. T. Gilbert, S. T. Fiske, & G. Linczey (Eds.), *Handbook of Social Psychology (4th ed.)*. New York, NY: Oxford University Press.

Zikmund, W. G., & Scott, J. E. (1973). A multivariate analysis of perceived risk, self-confidence, and information sources. In S. Ward & P. Wright (Eds.), *Advances in consumer research, proceedings of the 4th annual conference of the Association for Consumer Research* (pp. 406–416). Chicago, IL: Association of Consumer Research.

THE JOURNAL OF ENTREPRENEURIAL FINANCE VOLUME 16, NO. 2 (SPRING 2013) 33-56

Bank Loans to Newly Public Firms†

Sherrill Shaffer
University of Wyoming

Tatyana Sokolyk
Brock University

ABSTRACT

Prior studies have shown that newly public firms exhibit a high degree of uncertainty and asymmetric information, with few reliable sources of information. These findings suggest that investors could benefit if some independent party is able to assess the quality of a newly public firm. Since other studies have found that banks can reduce information asymmetry about firms that borrow, we examine whether banks provide information about the quality of newly public firms. We find that bank lending is consistently associated with positive long-term outcomes—newly public firms that borrow experience significantly smaller decreases in operating performance and better long-term stock performance than non-borrowers.

JEL Classification: G14, G21
Keywords: Newly public firms, Bank lending, IPO

I. Introduction

DESPITE THE FACT THAT THE INITIAL PUBLIC OFFERING (IPO) is a significant information-releasing event in the life of a firm, newly public firms experience a high degree of uncertainty and asymmetric information between the firm and investors, with few reliable sources of information (Teoh, Wong, and Rao, 1998). Several studies have documented that IPO firms, on average, generate positive abnormal stock returns in

†We are grateful to an anonymous referee and the editor for helpful comments and suggestions. We thank conference participants at the Financial Management Association meetings, Academy of Entrepreneurial Finance meetings, and Multinational Finance Association meetings for providing helpful comments on the earlier draft of this paper.

ISSN: 1551-9570

the short run but declining stock and operating performance in the long run (e.g., Loughran and Ritter, 1995). Furthermore, owners of a pre-IPO firm possess private information about the quality of the firm and may not truthfully disclose this information. Consistent with this notion, Ang and Brau (2002) show that IPO prospectuses are contaminated by optimistic bias, window dressing, and earnings manipulation. Teoh et al. (1998) report that newly public firms are more likely to engage in earnings management than are seasoned publicly traded firms. Moreover, analysts are overoptimistic about newly public firms and systematically overestimate their earnings (e.g., Dechow et al. 2000; Lin and McNichols, 1998; Michaely and Womack, 1999; Rajan and Servaes, 1997; Teoh and Wong, 2002).

The evidence in the studies highlighted above suggests that investors could benefit if some independent party were available to help assess the quality of a newly public firm. Theories of financial intermediation postulate that banks, through screening and monitoring associated with their lending activity, play a special role in reducing information asymmetry about firms that borrow (see Diamond 1984, 1991; Fama 1985; and Ramakrishan and Thakor1984). This study examines whether banks provide valuable information about the quality of newly public firms. Specifically, we examine whether bank lending to newly public firms is associated with better long-run performance in operating returns and stock returns.

We document a positive relation between bank lending and long-term performance of newly public firms. Generally, operating performance declines several years after an IPO.1 However, post-IPO borrowers experience significantly smaller declines in operating performance than do non-borrowers. Furthermore, post-IPO borrowers have better stock performance up to three years following the IPO. These findings suggest that banks perform an important role in certifying firm quality (identifying firms with better future prospects) and/or contributing to borrowers' subsequent performance through mechanisms identified in previous studies, such as monitoring or loan covenants (Diamond, 1984).

This study contributes to the existing literature in several ways. First, we document that bank loans serve as a significant source of funds for newly public firms. Second, we show that bank lending helps to reduce information asymmetry and

---

[1] Field and Karpoff (2002), Friedlan (1994), Jain and Kini (1994), and Mikkelson et al. (1997) also document post-IPO performance decline.

uncertainty about newly public firms. Third, we extend studies on bank lending to private and pre-IPO firms and show that the positive effect of bank lending continues in the post-IPO stage.

The remainder of the paper is organized as follows. The next section reviews related literature. Section III describes the data and examines differences in characteristics between post-IPO borrowers and non-borrowers. Section IV compares post-IPO operating and stock performance of borrowing and non-borrowing firms. Section V concludes the paper.

II. Literature Review

Accepted theories of financial intermediation postulate that banks acquire private information during the lending process (e.g., Berlin and Loeys, 1988; Bernanke, 1983; Diamond 1984, 1991; Fama, 1985). Leland and Pyle (1977) argue that the main reason for the existence of intermediaries is information asymmetry. Campbell and Kracaw (1980) argue that financial intermediaries produce information because the production of information and various intermediary services are naturally complimentary activities.[2]Overall, prior studies have concluded that banks use information-gathering and screening technology to produce information about a borrowing firm by thoroughly scrutinizing the borrower (e.g., Lummer and McConnell, 1989; Hauswald and Marquez, 2006). When a lending decision becomes publicly available, it therefore provides a favorable signal to the market about the future prospects of the borrowing firm.

In addition, banks undertake ongoing monitoring of borrowing firms while a loan is outstanding (Diamond, 1984; Fama, 1985). Such monitoring, combined with loan covenants and collateral requirements, helps to mitigate moral hazards and reduces the borrower's likelihood of default (Rajan and Winton, 1995). Monitoring by the lending bank is another reason why we might expect bank lending to be associated with improved subsequent operating performance of the borrower.

Theory thus indicates at least two mechanisms by which a bank loan can enhance a borrowing firm's value: screening, in which banks attempt to identify successful firms ex ante and monitoring, in which banks attempt to induce borrowing firms to achieve

---

[2]See also theoretical works by Black (1975), Kane and Malkiel (1965), Ramakrishan and Thakor (1984), and Boyd and Prescott (1986).

positive financial outcomes after the loan has been originated. Several empirical studies provide evidence that bank loans are "special" or "unique" by documenting positive abnormal returns to the announcements of bank loan agreements (e.g., James, 1987; Lummer and McConnell, 1989; Mikkelson and Partch, 1986).

The unique feature of our study is that we examine bank lending to newly public firms. In the empirical sections below, we test the hypothesis that bank loans are associated with improved subsequent operating performance. More recent studies have found positive effects of bank lending among private and pre-IPO firms (Schenone, 2004; Gonzalez and James, 2007; Benzoni and Schenone, 2010), whereas studies of seasoned public firms have found no such positive effects of bank lending (Billett et al. 2006; Fields et al. 2006). Reconciling these contrasting results is possible if the informational benefit of bank lending dissipates soon after a firm goes public. Such a pattern seems plausible because the IPO process generates and discloses new financial information about the firm. Therefore, by using data for newly public firms, we also shed new light on whether the pre-IPO benefits of bank lending identified in the prior literature vanish immediately upon going public or instead persist into the first years after the IPO. The next section describes our data and sample in more detail.

III. Sample Description

A. Data Sources and Sample Selection

We combine data from the following four sources: the Securities Data Corporation (SDC) New Issues database, the Dealscan database, the Center for Research and Security Prices (CRSP), and COMPUSTAT. The SDC New Issues database is utilized to identify U.S. common stock offerings during the period January 1, 1990 – December 31, 2000.[3] We eliminate closed-end funds, depositary shares, real estate investment trusts (REITs), spinoffs, unit issues, reverse leveraged buyouts, financial institutions (SIC codes 6000-6999), and utilities (SIC codes 4900-4999). We

[3] Our sample starts in 1990 because Dealscan has limited coverage of bank loans prior to the 1990s. Previous studies that document benefits of pre-IPO bank lending also end their samples in 2000(see, for example, Schenone, 2004; Gonzalez and James, 2007; Benzoni and Schenone, 2010).Thus, this time period allows us to draw comparisons and make connections with the existing literature on the positive effects of bank lending for young public firms.

also eliminate IPOs with offer prices below five dollars, and we check for the availability of post-IPO stock and accounting data on CRSP and COMPUSTAT, respectively. Previous IPO studies have used similar sample exclusion criteria (for example, Jain and Kini, 1994; Field and Karpoff, 2002; Gonzalez and James, 2007; Field and Lowry, 2009). Our final IPO sample contains 3,218 firms.

Data on the offer date, offer price, initial filing range, net IPO proceeds, and on whether the firm was backed by a venture capitalist are collected from SDC. For each firm, we also calculate the price run-up as the percentage difference between the offer price and the midpoint of the initial filing range. In addition, we compute the initial return as the percentage difference between the first after-market closing price and the offer price. We also record firm age, measured as the number of years since the company was founded.[4]

To determine which IPO firms receive bank loans soon after the initial public offering, we collect information on bank loans from the Dealscan database supplied by the Loan Pricing Corporation. Dealscan provides information on the characteristics and terms of bank loans, including the identity of the borrower and the lender and the date, type, amount, rate, and collateral of the loan. We restrict our sample to U.S. firms that borrowed from banks during the period January 1, 1990 – December 31, 2001, and we have loan year stock returns and accounting data on CRSP and COMPUSTAT, respectively. The sample period for loan deals is set at one year longer than the sample period for IPO firms to include information on loan deals for at least one year after the initial public offering in our analysis. To ensure that the abnormal "tech bubble" years do not influence our results, we check the robustness of our main findings by excluding firms that went public during 1998 – 2000; the results do not change qualitatively and are not reported for brevity.

Using Dealscan data, we collect information on the first bank loan to a newly public firm with the loan active date within one year from the IPO offer date. Out of 3,218 IPO firms, 765 had a loan agreement within one year from the initial public offering. One-third of these loan deals occurred during the first quarter after the IPO date. Hereinafter, firms that borrow from banks within one year after the IPO date are called "post-IPO borrowers." Firms that do not borrow within one year after the IPO

[4] We thank Laura Field for providing firm age data. These data come from various sources and are described in Field and Lowry (2009, footnote 2).

are labeled "non-borrowers." Table I presents a summary of the variable definitions and sources of data.

B. Summary Statistics

Table II reports sample descriptive statistics on the number of IPOs, the IPO offer characteristics, the number of post-IPO borrowers, and on bank loan characteristics, aggregated across the total sample and by IPO year. The average firm in the sample raised about US$50 million in net IPO proceeds and experienced a first-day return of about 26 percent. The median firm raised more than US$26 million, with a median initial return of 10 percent. The time trends in the number of IPOs, IPO proceeds, and initial IPO returns are consistent with those of previous studies

Table I
Variable Definitions and Data Sources

Firm Characteristics	*Source: All variables, unless stated otherwise, are from COMPUSTAT Industrial Annual*
Total Assets	data6
Sales	data12
Total Debt /Total Assets	leverage ratio = (data9+data5)/data6
PPE /Total Assets	tangible assets =ratio of property, plan equipment to total assets = data7/data6
ROA	return on assets = ratio of net income to total assets = data13/data6
Inventory / Total Assets	data3/data6
Tobin's Q	market value of equity plus total debt, divided by total assets =(data24*data25+data9+data5)/data6
Age	firm age (in years) from the date of incorporation to the IPO date; see Field and Lowry (2009) for explanation of data sources.
Tech Industry	an indicator variable that equals 1 for firms in the technology industry (based on four digit SIC codes listed in Loughran and Ritter, 2004) and equals 0 otherwise
Offer Characteristics	*Source: SDC New Issues database*

Net IPO Proceeds	the amount raised by a firm through the initial public offering, minus the total fees paid, adjusted for inflation and reported in millions of real 1990 dollars
VC-backed	an indicator variable that equals 1 if an IPO firm was backed by a venture capitalist at the time of IPO and equals 0 otherwise
Price Run-up	the percentage difference between the offer price and the midpoint of the initial filing range
Initial Return	the percentage difference between the first after-market closing price (from CRSP) and the offer price
Loan Characteristics	*Source: Dealscan*
Loan Amount	the amount borrowed from a bank, adjusted for inflation and reported in millions of real 1990 dollars
All-In Spread Drawn	measures the amount the borrower pays in basis points over LIBOR for each dollar drawn down and includes the spread of the loan and any annual or facility fee paid to the bank
Syndicate	an indicator variable that equals 1 if more than one bank was involved in loan agreement and equals 0 otherwise

and show a well-documented pattern that IPOs in the period from the late 1990s to the early 2000s were large IPOs with high first-day returns (see Loughran and Ritter, 2004; Ritter and Welch, 2002).

It is striking that, despite the funds raised in an IPO, many newly public firms draw on bank financing. In the sample of 3,218 U.S. firms that went public during 1990 – 2000, almost one-quarter (764, or 24 percent) borrowed from banks at least once during their first year of public trading. The average loan amount was $84 million, which is 1.7 times the average amount raised through the initial public offering. The median loan amount was more than $30 million, which is also larger than the median $26 million raised by a firm through an IPO. Overall, banks contributed a significant portion to the financing mix of newly public firms, with the loan amount exceeding the net IPO proceeds by 44 percent. These statistics suggest that a significant portion of newly public firms rely heavily on bank loans soon after the initial public offering.

The time trends in loan frequency and loan characteristics are also noteworthy. By the end of the sample period, which was characterized by large IPO proceeds and high initial returns, the proportion of IPO firms receiving bank loans dropped to less than 13 percent. Firms borrowed large amounts during those years, with the mean loan

Table II
Sample Descriptive Statistics

The sample includes 3,218 U.S. firms that went public during 1990-2000. *Post-IPO Borrowers* are 765 firms that borrow from banks within one year from the firm's IPO. IPO data are from SDC, bank loan data are from Dealscan, and stock performance data are from CRSP. *Net IPO Proceeds* and *Loan Amount* are adjusted for inflation and are reported in millions of real 1990 dollars. Variable definitions are provided in Table I.

		IPO Offer Characteristics			Bank Loan Characteristics		
IPO Year	Number of IPOs	Net IPO Proceeds Mean [Median]	Initial Return Mean [Median]	Number of post-IPO Borrowers	Loan Amount Mean [Median]	Loan Amount/ Net IPO Proceeds Mean [Median]	All-In Spread Drawn Mean [Median]
1990	68	37.33	8.08	19	85.59	1.59	201.25
		[23.43]	[5.72]		[20.00]	[0.88]	[255.00]
1991	175	42.20	12.13	41	91.19	1.20	234.71
		[24.94]	[7.50]		[15.33]	[0.62]	[255.00]
1992	270	38.98	10.76	70	46.78	1.10	241.21
		[22.40]	[4.36]		[23.16]	[0.85]	[250.00]
1993	350	33.74	12.07	101	63.61	1.32	209.46
		[22.46]	[6.13]		[35.78]	[0.94]	[200.00]
1994	291	29.38	9.84	72	67.23	1.36	187.78
		[19.33]	[4.81]		[32.13]	[1.23]	[175.00]
1995	322	40.65	21.00	67	110.47	1.48	199.67
		[24.70]	[12.54]		[23.35]	[0.67]	[200.00]
1996	476	41.22	16.83	127	100.78	1.93	209.68
		[25.97]	[10.00]		[30.38]	[0.98]	[200.00]
1997	355	39.34	13.67	113	68.08	1.38	186.44
		[23.69]	[8.90]		[23.16]	[1.00]	[175.00]
1998	214	77.02	23.16	61	139.00	2.02	192.26
		[26.78]	[9.47]		[56.47]	[1.33]	[175.00]
1999	383	77.25	72.98	54	156.73	0.95	212.08
		[37.34]	[38.75]		[39.89]	[0.50]	[212.50]
2000	314	84.76	58.09	40	181.36	0.95	256.69
		[43.31]	[28.14]		[33.78]	[0.52]	[255.00]
10-Year Averages		49.59	25.93		84.05	1.44	208.00
		[26.47]	[10.00]		[30.31]	[0.91]	[200.00]
Totals	3,218			765			

amount peaking at $181 million (median = $34 million) in 2000. However, the loan amounts were smaller relative to net IPO proceeds during those years than in any prior year. Furthermore, the loan cost was relatively high at the end of the sample period. The mean loan cost, measured by "all-in spread drawn," was 208 points (median = 200) for the overall sample and reached 257 basis points (median = 255) in 2000.[5]

These statistics show that fewer IPO firms borrowed from banks during the "tech bubble" years (1998 – 2000), but those firms that did borrow during those years paid higher interest rates. This pattern could indicate that many firms did not need bank loans during those years since they were able to raise large amounts through an IPO. An alternative explanation is that banks were more selective during "hot IPO" years. They loaned to fewer IPO firms, offered smaller amounts relative to net IPO proceeds, and charged higher interest rates.

In non-tabulated analysis, we examine the distribution of loans by loan purpose, loan structure, and firms' credit rating and find the following patterns. The most frequently stated purpose of a loan is general corporate purpose (35 percent of loans), followed by debt repayment (25 percent) and working capital needs (16 percent). Sixty percent of post-IPO loans are secured. The Standard and Poor's credit rating at the close of the loan deal is A-AAA for 1.4 percent of the firms, B-BBB for 12.9 percent of the firms, and is not available for 85 percent of the sample firms.

C. Borrowers versus Non-Borrowers

Table III compares characteristics of post-IPO borrowers and non-borrowers. All accounting measures are from COMPUSTAT for the year immediately prior to the IPO year. Since about one third of post-IPO borrowers receive loans within three months of the initial public offering, the arbitrary choice of a pre-IPO year ensures that

---

[5] "All-in spread drawn," reported by Dealscan, measures the amount the borrower pays in basis points over the London InterBank Offered Rate (LIBOR) for each dollar drawn down, and includes the spread of the loan and any annual or facility fee paid to the bank group.

firms' characteristics are not affected by the bank loan examined in the following analysis. Data prior to their IPO year are not available on 178 firms.[6]

Table III shows that post-IPO borrowers are quite different from non-borrowers. They are much larger (as measured by the firms' assets and sales), have higher leverage (measured by the ratio of debt to assets), and carry a higher level of inventory relative to total assets. Post-IPO borrowers are more profitable (measured by return on assets) and invest more in tangible assets (measured by the ratio of property, plant, and equipment to total assets).

Offer characteristics also differ between post-IPO borrowers and non-borrowers. Post-IPO borrowers have been in business longer at the time they go public, are less likely to be backed by venture capitalists, and are less likely to operate in the technology industry. Post-IPO borrowers also have lower initial returns.

In summary, this section documents that a significant portion of newly public firms borrow large amounts from banks soon after the initial public offering. The firm and IPO characteristics of post-IPO borrowers are quite different from those of non-borrowers. The next section examines whether bank lending is associated with better performance of newly public firms.

IV. Post-IPO Borrowers versus Non-Borrowers: Post-IPO Performance

Fama (1985) argues that banks may enhance a borrowing firm's value by reducing information asymmetry or by monitoring firm performance. We investigate whether bank lending within one year after the initial public offering is associated with better subsequent operating and long-term stock performance.[7] This setting allows us to examine whether banks enhance the performance of borrowing firms in an environment with high information production by public sources and also with a high degree of uncertainty about future firm performance.

---

[6] Of these, 38 firms borrowed from the banks within one year of their IPO date. For these 178 firms, we collect accounting variables for the IPO year. The main results do not change if we omit these firms from the analysis.

[7] In unreported analysis, we find no differences in survival rates between post-IPO borrowers and non-borrowers. This suggests that we do not encounter a survivorship bias when comparing the long-term performance of borrowers and non-borrowers.

Table III
Differences in Firm and Offer Characteristics between Post-IPO Borrowers and Non-Borrowers

The sample includes 3,218 U.S. firms that went public during 1990-2000. *Post-IPO Borrowers* are the 765 firms that borrowed from banks within one year of the firm's IPO. IPO data are from SDC, bank loan data are from Dealscan, accounting data are from COMPUSTAT, and stock performance data are from CRSP. All accounting variables are measured at the fiscal year-end immediately prior to the IPO year. Variable definitions are provided in Table I.

Characteristics	Overall Sample Mean [Median]	Post-IPO Borrowers Mean [Median]	Non-Borrowers Mean [Median]	*t*-statistic for the difference in Means [Medians]
Total Assets (1990 real $, mln)	169.27	447.44	82.51	364.93***
	[18.08]	[47.28]	[14.52]	[32.76]***
Sales (1990 real $, mln)	155.52	378.87	85.86	293.01***
	[20.71]	[52.70]	[15.33]	[37.37]***
Total Debt / Total Assets	0.60	0.67	0.58	0.09***
	[0.56]	[0.65]	[0.52]	[0.14] ***
PPE / Total Assets	0.36	0.44	0.33	0.11***
	[0.26]	[0.35]	[0.24]	[0.11] ***
ROA	-0.05	0.11	-0.10	0.21***
	[0.11]	[0.15]	[0.09]	[0.05] ***
Inventory / Total Assets	0.12	0.16	0.11	0.05***
	[0.04]	[0.07]	[0.03]	[0.04]***

Table III
(continued)

Characteristics	Overall Sample Mean [Median]	Post-IPO Borrowers Mean [Median]	Non-Borrowers Mean [Median]	*t*-statistic for the difference in Means [Medians]
Age	13.55	18.08	12.10	5.98***
	[7.00]	[9.00]	[7.00]	[2.00]***
VC-backed	0.42	0.31	0.46	0.14***
	[0.00]	[0.00]	[0.00]	
Tech Industry	0.21	0.10	0.25	-0.15***
	[0.00]	[0.00]	[0.00]	
Initial Return (%)	25.93	16.41	28.90	-12.48***
	[10.00]	[7.50]	[10.71]	[-3.21]***
Price Run-Up (%)	-1.48	-4.22	-0.63	-3.59***
	[0.00]	[0.00]	[0.00]	[0.00]***

*** and **indicate significance at the 1% and 5% levels, respectively.

Our model and data have several intrinsic limitations. Like other studies in the literature, we cannot establish causality between bank lending and firms' financial outcomes. Similarly, we cannot identify whether any observed differences in performance between borrowers and non-borrowers are attributed to banks' screening activities versus monitoring or loan covenants. Finally, we cannot observe the demand for bank loans, and thus cannot say whether non-borrowing firms were denied bank credit or did not need to borrow. Other studies of bank lending have all faced these or similar limitations (Lummer and McConnell, 1989; Billett et al. 2006; Gonzalez and James, 2007; Benzoni and Schenone, 2010).

A. Changes in Operating Performance after the IPO

We first investigate whether a firm's post-IPO operating performance is related to its borrowing soon after the initial public offering. Operating performance is measured as operating return on assets (ROA), which equals operating income divided by the book value of total assets. We examine both raw and industry-adjusted changes in ROA measured from the IPO year through each of the five years following the IPO. The raw change in ROA for IPO firm *i* from the year of the IPO (year 0) to year *t* is

$$\Delta ROA_{i,(0,t)} = ROA_{i,t} - ROA_{i,0} \quad (1)$$

The industry-adjusted change in ROA controls for the contemporaneous change in firm *i*'s industry ROA and is measured as firm *i*'s change in ROA minus the industry median change in ROA on the same date. The industries are based on the most disaggregated SIC category containing at least five non-IPO firms, up to four-digit SIC codes.[8] The industry-adjusted change in ROA for IPO firm *i* from the year of the IPO (year 0) to year *t* is:

[8] That is, we use four-digit SIC codes for industries containing at least five non-IPO firms, or three-digit SIC codes if there are at least five non-IPO firms at the three-digit level but not at the four-digit level. We use two-digit SIC codes if the three-digit level contains fewer than five non-issuing firms.

$$\text{Adjusted } \Delta ROA_{i,(0,t)} = (ROA_{i,t} - ROA_{i,0}) - (\text{Industry Median } ROA_{i,t} - \text{Industry Median } ROA_{i,0}) \quad (2)$$

Data to compute changes in ROA through the first post-IPO year are available for 2,906 IPO firms, declining to 1,723 firms for a five-year change in ROA.

Table IV reports mean values of raw and industry-adjusted changes in ROA measured through each of the five years following the IPO. Consistent with prior studies, operating performance declines over all time intervals examined (see Field and Karpoff, 2002; Friedlan, 1994; Jain and Kini, 1994; Mikkelson et al. 1997). As shown in Panel A, the mean change in the raw ROA from the IPO year to the following year is –0.051, with a *t*-statistic of –12.45. The mean change from the IPO year through the following two years is –0.069, with a *t*-statistic of –13.46. The average change in raw ROA remains around –0.06 through years 3, 4, and 5.

Panel B shows that industry-adjusted changes in ROA are also significantly negative for the first five years after the IPO. From the IPO year to the following year, the industry-adjusted change in ROA is –0.039 with a *t*-statistic of –9.20. From the IPO year to years 2 and 3, the industry-adjusted change in ROA is about –0.05, leveling off to about –0.040 for years 4 and 5 after the IPO.

Table IV further reports differences in raw and industry-adjusted changes in operating performance between post-IPO borrowers and non-borrowers. Within three years after the IPO, changes in operating performance tend to be less negative for firms that borrow from banks within one year after the IPO than for other firms. For example, from the IPO to the following year, the mean industry-adjusted change in ROA is –0.046 for non-borrowing firms, compared to –0.016 for borrowing firms. This difference is statistically significant at the 1 percent level, and decreases starting in year 3 after the IPO. By year 5, this difference disappears. This suggests that banks are "special" in the sense that they are able to identify firms with better future prospects and/or contribute to better operating performance of post-IPO borrowers through monitoring, loan covenants, or related mechanisms.

Table V provides additional support for this finding. It reports the results of ordinary least squares (OLS) regression of industry-adjusted changes in ROA on the presence of post-IPO loan and other firm characteristics, measured through two years after the initial public offering. *Post-IPO Loan* is an indicator variable that equals 1 if a firm borrows from a bank within one year after its IPO, and equals 0 otherwise. Other

Table V
OLS Regression of Post-IPO Changes in Operating Performance

The sample includes 2,228 U.S. firms that went public during 1990-2000. The dependent variable is *Change in Industry-Adjusted ROA*, measured from the IPO year through 2 years post-IPO. *Industry-Adjusted ROA* is defined as net income divided by total assets for the IPO firm minus the industry median net income divided by total assets on the same date, where the industries are based on 4-digit SIC codes if there is a minimum of at least 5 non-issuing firms, else 3-digit SIC codes, or 2-digit SIC codes. *Post-IPO Loan* equals 1 if an IPO firm borrows from a bank within the first year after going public, and it equals 0 otherwise. IPO year dummy variables are included in the regression but not reported. IPO data are from SDC, bank loan data are from Dealscan, accounting data are from COMPUSTAT, and stock performance data are from CRSP. *t*-statistics are provided in parentheses.

Variable	Coefficient Estimate
Intercept	-0.219
	(-5.52)***
Post-IPO Loan	0.030
	(2.41)**
Tobin's Q	0.010
	(5.02)***
Ln (Net IPO Proceeds)	0.015
	(2.58)**
Ln (1+Age)	0.005
	(0.94)
Initial Return	0.000
	(0.87)
VC-backed	0.008
	(0.73)
Adjusted R^2(%)	2.34

*** and ** indicate significance at the 1% and 5% levels, respectively.

Table VI
Buy-and-Hold Returns One, Two and Three Years after the IPO

The sample includes 3,218 U.S. firms that went public during 1990-2000. *Post-IPO Borrowers* are firms that borrow from banks within one year of the firm's IPO. *Non-Borrowers* are firms that do not borrow from banks within one year of the firm's IPO. *BH Raw Returns* are buy-and-hold firm returns, in percent. *BHVW* are buy-and-hold firm returns, in percentages, adjusted for contemporaneous CRSP value-weighted returns. *BHEW* are buy-and-hold firm returns, in percentages, adjusted for contemporaneous CRSP equally weighted returns. All returns are measured through 1, 2, and 3 years after a firm's IPO. IPO data are from SDC, bank loan data are from Dealscan, accounting data are from COMPUSTAT, and stock performance data are from CRSP.

Performance Measure	Post-IPO Borrowers	Non-Borrowers	Difference
1-year post-IPO			
BH Raw Returns	117.96	103.82	-14.14***
BHVW	2.29	-9.18	-11.47***
BHEW	5.35	-9.17	-14.52***
2-years post-IPO			
BH Raw Returns	133.40	112.39	-21.00***
BHVW	-0.16	-14.34	-14.18*
BHEW	5.71	-13.87	-19.58**
3-years post-IPO			
BH Raw Returns	134.49	119.61	-14.88*
BHVW	-14.93	-20.17	-5.23
BHEW	-6.50	-18.11	-11.61

***, **, and * indicate significance at the 1%, 5%, and 10% levels, respectively.

Table VII provides additional support for this finding. It reports the results of an ordinary least squares regression of the two-year buy-and-hold abnormal return (adjusted for the value-weighted CRSP return) on the presence of a post-IPO loan and other firm characteristics. The coefficient on *Post-IPO Loan* is positive and significant at the 1 percent level. Consistent with the evidence presented in Table VI, this result indicates that borrowing from a bank soon after the IPO is associated with positive long-term stock performance. This long-term stock effect is consistent with the pattern of long-term operating performance reported in Table V.

Table VII
OLS Regression of Abnormal Returns Two Years after the IPO

The sample includes 3,218 U.S. firms that went public during 1990-2000. The dependent variable is a firm's buy-and-hold abnormal return, adjusted for contemporaneous CRSP value-weighted return, measured through two years following the initial public offering. *Post-IPO Loan* equals 1 if a firm borrows from a bank within the first year after going public, and it equals 0 otherwise. IPO year dummy variables are included in the regression but not reported. IPO data are from SDC, bank loan data are from Dealscan, accounting data are from COMPUSTAT, and stock performance data are from CRSP. Definitions of other variables are provided in Table I. *t*-statistics are provided in parentheses.

Variable	Coefficient Estimate
Intercept	-0.925
	(-2.86)***
Post-IPO Loan	0.343
	(3.37)***
Tobin's Q	0.313
	(18.31)***
Ln (Net IPO Proceeds)	0.014
	(0.30)
Ln (1+Age)	-0.010
	(-0.25)
Initial Return	-0.001
	(-1.42)
VC-backed	0.220
	(2.47)**
Adjusted R^2 (%)	15.91

*** and ** indicate significance at the 1% and 5%levels, respectively.

V. Conclusion

Motivated by prior findings that newly public firms are characterized by a high degree of uncertainty, high information asymmetry between the firm and investors, and the few reliable sources of information, we examine whether banks provide valuable information about the quality of newly public firms. The main findings can be summarized as follows. Bank lending is consistently associated with positive long-term outcomes. Post-IPO borrowers, on average, experience significantly smaller decreases in operating performance than non-borrowers up to three years after the IPO. Likewise, firms that borrow from banks within one year after an IPO experience better long-term stock performance, on average up to three years after the IPO.[9] This pattern is consistent with the ability of banks to reduce the degree of asymmetric information by some combination of screening applicants and/or monitoring borrowers' actions, although our data cannot evaluate the relative contribution of these two mechanisms. In either case, bank loans appear to be special for newly public firms, consistent with recent findings for pre-IPO firms and in contrast to recent findings for seasoned firms.

REFERENCES

Ang, James S. and James C. Brau, 2002, "Firm Transparency and the Costs of Going Public", Journal of Financial Research 1, 1-17.

Benzoni, Luca and Carola Schenone, 2010, "Conflict of Interest and Certification: Long-Term Performance and Valuation of U.S. IPOs Underwritten by Relationship Banks", Journal of Financial Intermediation 19, 235-254.

Berlin, Mitchell and Jan Loeys, 1988, "Bond Covenants and Delegated Monitoring", Journal of Finance 43, 397-412.

---

[9] Of course, this does not mean that *every* post-IPO borrower experiences outcomes superior to every non-borrower, nor does it imply that banks can perfectly identify superior performers ex ante.

Bernanke, Ben S., 1983, "Nonmonetary Effects of the Financial Crisis in Propagation of the Great Depression", American Economic Review 73, 257-276.

Billett, Matthew T., Mark J. Flannery, and Jon A. Garfinkel, 2006, "Are Bank Loans Special? Evidence on the Post Announcement Performance of Bank Borrowers", Journal of Financial and Quantitative Analysis 41, 733-751.

Black, Fischer, 1975, "Banks Funds Management in an Efficient Market", Journal of Financial Economics 2, 323-340.

Boyd, John H. and Edward C. Prescott, 1986, "Financial Intermediary-coalitions", Journal of Economic Theory 38, 211-232.

Campbell, Tim S. and William A. Kracaw, 1980, "Information Production, Market Signaling, and the Theory of Financial Intermediation", Journal of Finance 35, 863-882.

Dechow, Patricia M., Amy P. Hutton, and Richard G. Sloan, 2000, "The Relation Between Analysts' Forecasts of Long-Term Earnings Growth and Stock Price Performance Following Equity Offerings", Contemporary Accounting Research 17, 1-32.

Diamond, Douglas W., 1984, "Financial Intermediation and Delegated Monitoring", Review of Economic Studies 51, 393-414.

Diamond, Douglas W., 1991, "Monitoring and Reputation: The Choice between Bank Loans and Directly Placed Debt", Journal of Political Economy 99, 689-721.

Fama, Eugene F., 1985, "What's Different about Banks?",Journal of Monetary Economics 10, 10-19.

Field, Laura C. and Jonathan M. Karpoff, 2002, "Takeover Defenses of IPO Firms", Journal of Finance 57, 1857-1889.

Field, Laura C. and Michelle Lowry, 2009, "Institutional Versus Individual Investments in IPOs: The Importance of Firm Fundamentals", Journal of Financial and Quantitative Analysis 44, 489-516.

Fields, L. Paige, Donald R. Fraser, Tammy L. Berry, and Steven Byers, 2006, "Do Bank Loan Relationships Still Matter?",Journal of Money, Credit, and Banking 38, 1195-1209.

Friedlan, Jogn M., 1994, "Accounting Choices of Issuers of Initial Public Offerings", Contemporary Accounting Research 11, 1-23.

Gonzalez, Laura and Christopher James, 2007, "Banks and Bubbles: How Good are Bankers at Spotting Winners?", Journal of Financial Economics 86, 40-70.

Hauswald, Robert and Robert Maequez, 2006, "Competition and Strategic Information Acquisition in Credit Markets", Review of Financial Studies 19, 967-1000.

Jain, Bharat A. and Omesh Kini, 1994, "The Post-Issue Operating Performance of IPO Firms", Journal of Finance 49, 1699-1726.

James, Christopher, 1987, "Some Evidence of the Uniqueness of Bank Loans", Journal of Financial Economics 19, 217-235.

Kane, Edward J., and Burton G. Malkiel, 1965, "Bank Portfolio Allocation, Deposit Variability, and the Availability Doctrine", Quarterly Journal of Economics 79, 113-134.

Leland, Hayne E. and David H. Pyle, 1977, "Information Asymmetries, Financial Structure and Financial Intermediaries", Journal of Finance 32, 371-387.

Lin, Hsiou-wei and Maureen F. McNichols, 1998, "Underwriting Relationships, Analysts' Earnings Forecasts and Investment Recommendations", Journal of Accounting and Economics25, 101–127.

Loughran, Tim and Jay R. Ritter, 1995, "The New Issues Puzzle", Journal of Finance 50, 23-52.

Loughran, Tim and Jay R. Ritter, 2004, "Why has IPO Underpricing Increased Over Time?", Financial Management 33, 5-37.

Lummer, Scott L. and John J. McConnell, 1989, "Further Evidence on the Bank Lending Process and the Capital Market Response to the Bank Loan Agreements", Journal of Financial Economics 25, 99-122.

Michaely, Roni and Kent L. Womack, 1999, "Conflict of Interest and the Credibility of Underwriter Analysts Recommendations", Review of Financial Studies12, 653–686.

Mikkelson, Wayne H. and M. Megan Partch, 1986, "Valuation Effects of Securities Offerings and the Issuance Process", Journal of Financial Economics 15, 31-60.

Mikkelson, Wayne H., M. Megan Partch, and Kshitij Shah, 1997, "Ownership and Operating Performance of Companies that Go Public", Journal of Financial Economics 44, 281-307.

Rajan, Raghuram and Henri Servaes, 1997, "Analyst Following of Initial Public Offerings", Journal of Finance 52, 507-529.

Rajan, Raghuram and Andrew Winton, 1995, "Covenants and Collateral as Incentives to Monitor", Journal of Finance 50, 1113-1146.

Ramakrishan, Ram T.S. and Anjan V. Thakor, 1984, "Information Reliability and a Theory of Financial Intermediation", Review of Economic Studies 51, 415-432.

Ritter, Jay R. and Ivo Welch, 2002, "A Review of IPO Activity, Pricing, and Allocations", Journal of Finance 57, 1795-1828.

Schenone, Carola, 2004, "The Effect of Banking Relationships on the Firm's Cost of Equity in its IPO", Journal of Finance 59, 2901- 2958.

Teoh, Siew H., Ivo Welch, and T.J. Wong, 1998, "Earnings Management and the Long-run Performance of Initial Public Offerings", Journal of Finance 53, 1935-1974.

Teoh, Siew H. and T.J. Wong, 2002, "Why New Issues and High-Accrual Firms Underperform: The Role of Analysts' Credulity", Review of Financial Studies 15, 869-900.

Teoh, Siew H., T.J. Wong, and Gita R. Rao, 1998, "Are Accruals During Initial Public Offerings Opportunistic?", Review of Accounting Studies 3, 175-208.

THE JOURNAL OF ENTREPRENEURIAL FINANCE VOLUME 16, NO. 2 (SPRING 2013) 57-74

A Robust Valuation Model for Entrepreneurial Ventures

Haim Kedar-Levy[1]
Ben Gurion University of the Negev, and Ono Academic College

ABSTRACT

Pro forma estimation of financial statements often builds on constant ratios to sales revenue. While constant ratios may be relevant for established firms operating in predictable industries, they yield non-informative and possibly misleading information when applied to new firms, and particularly to technology ventures. Because new firms grow and change rapidly, a robust analysis should be based on intimate familiarity with the specific firm's business plan. This paper presents an alternative approach that links the firm's budget, as derived from its business plan, to pro forma financial statements, and to valuation models. The resulting estimated firm value is less sensitive to exogenous parameter assumptions than other methodologies.

JEL Classification: G17, G32, L26, M13.
Key words: Valuation; Business plan; Entrepreneurship; Pro forma financial statements.

I. Introduction

A COMMON APPROACH TO MODELING PRO FORMA financial statements is assuming constant ratios of expense and capital spending to sales revenue, or to items in the balance sheet (Arnold and James, 2000), in accordance with industry averages. Among the more important parameters that enter into such models are the exogenous assumptions on the annual growth rate of sales and the ratio of cost of goods sold (COGS) to sales. While this approach may be relevant to mature firms, in the case of new technology firms a smart choice of parameters may present almost any firm as

---

[1] Senior Lecturer of Finance at the Guilford Glazer Faculty of Business and Management, Ben Gurion University of the Negev, and Ono Academic College. T- (972)-8-647-2569, F-(972)-2-579-5678, hlevy@som.bgu.ac.il

ISSN: 1551-9570

extremely profitable. Indeed, during the internet bubble of the late 1990s, researchers questioned whether those new-technology firms were valued in a manner that is related to traditional financial statements (Core, Guay, and Van Buskirk, 2003, Trueman, Wong, and Zhang, 2000). Evidently, throughout the early stages of introducing a new technology to the market, the interactions between financial statement variables do not obey linear and predictable rules. Rather, they are often the result of activities that do not characterize mature firms, such as allocating more resources to research and development than to production or marketing, or up-scaling production and sales by tens or even hundreds of percent. Whenever a financial ratio varies considerably over time, a pro forma analysis based on its assumed consistency becomes non-informative. To accommodate this issue we present a different approach, which builds on a generic budget model of operations and capital. By explicitly representing the financial implications of specific business-plan activities into the budget model, the analyst measures their profitability implications for the venture, irrespective of linearity assumptions. We argue that because the resulting budget represents firm-specific operations, and because the pro forma financial statements and valuations are mostly driven from the budget, the end result is highly robust.

The problem of rapidly changing financial ratios, sales growth rates, and profitability measures of new technology firms has been modeled by Schwartz and Moon (2000, 2001), who applied a real-options approach in a simplified, stochastic pro forma model. Their model allows for periodic changes in the expected growth rate of sales, to its standard deviation, and to other variables. It yields a path-dependent valuation model, which, after calibration and estimation, yields a rational pricing model. Our focus is intentionally tilted to preferring an insider-out perspective, (i.e., we assume that the analyst knows the firm and its management, strategy, and capabilities, and she or he follows a consistent business plan). Schwartz and Moon (2003) acknowledge the need to be highly informed of the specific firm, at least in estimating the model parameters[2]. An additional difference between our approaches is the sensitivity to initial conditions. Schwartz and Moon (2000) estimate firm value through the stochastic simulation approach, as if an outsider analyst is observing the firm's reported data and simulates its possible paths of evolution. By so doing, they find

---

[2] When discussing the need to estimate the model parameters, Schwartz and Moon (2000) write: "*The determination of some parameters, however, requires the use of judgment, which can come only from a thorough knowledge of the specific situation*", *p. 64.*

that valuation is highly sensitive to the estimated benchmark parameters. This path-dependency problem is minimized by using our approach, because path dependency evolves through the implementation of the business plan, rather than an outsider's statistical projection of past performance.

Our model is made of three key sections, and is readily representable on a worksheet. For this reason we present some of the equations, especially those involving IF statements, in an Excel format[3]. The first section presents a generic budget model built from a firm's business plan. The second section contains the pro forma financial statements, which, aside from a few parameters, are directly derived from the budget model. The interactions between the balance sheet (BS) and the profit and loss (P&L) statements are solved recursively and solve, for the net profit. The third section converts the estimated net profit to free cash flow. It then allows the analyst to modify equity capital requirements, as well as long-term debt, such that the accumulated free cash flow remains positive at a satisfactory level. This section ends with a robust valuation model, which incorporates the estimated free cash flows, three alternative models for terminal value estimation, and allows the analyst to conduct sensitivity analyses to relevant parameters.

The rest of the paper describes the budget model in Section II, the pro forma statements in Section III, and the valuation part in Section IV. Section V presents conclusions and insights to the papers' contributions to analysts and the literature.

II. Generic budget model

The budget structure is presented in Exhibit 1. It is made of twelve tables, some of which serve to collect input data, while others are calculated from inputs or calculations. All tables can be thought of as matrixes relevant for the enterprise being evaluated. Tables 1 – 6 have dimensions mXn, where m=number of products, or sources of revenue, and n=estimation periods (normally 0,1,...,5). Tables 7 – 9 present manpower cost, and have dimensions qXn, where q=number of employee groups. It is important to distinguish and summarize separately the list of employees denoted as "Direct Labor" from those denoted "Indirect Labor." While the former is part of

[3] Interested readers may obtain the model on an Excel file from the author through email: hlevy@som.bgu.ac.il

operating expenses in the P&L, the latter constitutes general, administrative, research and development, and marketing expenses. This distinction therefore allows one to form more accurate profitability measures of the firm. It should be noted that this important distinction is absent from existing models.

Table 10 includes as many expense items as needed to appropriately represent the structure of the sales and marketing expenses in the firm. While some of the expense items are simple inputs, others may be a fraction of sales (possibly of specific products) depending on the firm's commission agreements with its sales force. Table 11 lists all general and administrative expenses, and Table 12 lists capital expenditure items. All tables should have a table-specific summary line (a vector of 1Xn) that will later feed into the financial statements.

Exhibit 1
Description of the different tables of the budget model

Table 1:	Input expected unit sales, by product
Table 2:	Input average selling price per unit, by product
Table 3:	Items in Table 1 times corresponding items in Table 2
Table 4:	Input variable cost per unit (excluding direct labor cost), by product
Table 5:	Items in Table 1 times corresponding items in Table 4
Table 6:	Items in Table 3 minus corresponding items in Table 5
Table 7:	Manpower requirements, direct and indirect, by positions (1=100%)
Table 8:	Input average position cost to employer, including all social benefits and taxes
Table 9:	Items in Table 7 times corresponding items in Table 8
Table 10:	Row Vector #1: Expected percentage commission paid on sales. (optional)
	Row Vector #2: Items in Row Vector #1 times total sales[3] (optional)
	Additional row vectors: Specific marketing expenditure items as needed
Table 11:	Input relevant G&A expense items
Table 12:	Input relevant additions to fixed assets per year (period).

There are two key advantages to this generic budget model. First, the budget details are verifiable across several dimensions, and therefore enable a robust valuation methodology. For example, the forecast of unit sales can, and should, be verified by the sales and marketing department, making sure they can allocate the sales force and meet sales projections. Further, it should be coordinated with the manufacturing department, making sure the items can be produced given the planned production capacity. Consistently, the capital budget must reflect the deployment of production capabilities with the relevant lead-time, and so on. Second, the different tables of the model constitute all the expected expense and capital budgets of the firm, and therefore they can be mapped directly into the financial statements. This is advantageous because the analyst need not estimate market share percentages and\or growth rates of sales.

III. Pro forma financial statements

A. Parameters

Our BS and P&L statements are built primarily from data drawn from the budget, and to a lesser extent from data in Exhibit 2 below. The budget feeds the most important items in the P&L (i.e., those items that determine a significant part of each period's profit or loss). Before delving into the detailed equations of the model, it is important to be aware of several parameters that determine a few items in the BS. We take all these parameters as time varying, albeit the impact that some of them have on the period's profit and loss, and consequently on firm's valuation, are negligible.

The first parameter of Exhibit 2 represents a fiscal policy assumption concerning the government's expected corporate tax rates. Alternatively, if the firm is eligible for reduced tax rates for some reason this assumption can be reflected in a similar manner. Next, the firm's dividend policy, contingent on positive net profit, should be listed throughout the pro forma years. The contingent leverage policy of the firm, which may be realized if the firm's equity capital (Equity stock + Retained earnings) is positive, is determined by the ratio of the third row.

The rest of the parameters represent expected ratios of the firm with respect to sales, such as the ratios of receivables, inventory, or payables. In the long run these ratios would normally converge to industry norms. Depreciation rate represents the weighted average rate of depreciation on the firm's fixed assets. Rates of interest on credit balances and short- and long-term debt should be entered based on expectations. The average maturity of long-term debt is used to calculate principal payments.

B. The balance sheet

Our balance sheet is intentionally simple in terms of the number of items it is built of, serving to minimize the number of exogenous parameters in the financial statements. However, unlike other models that use a single "plug equation" to balance the balance sheet (e.g., Copeland, Koller, and Murrin, 1994, Benninga and Sarig, 1997, Arnold and James, 2000), our BS incorporates two "plug equations." Our first plug equation calculates "Cash and Bank Deposits," and the second calculates "Short Term Debt." The reason is that if one is positive, the other is essentially zero. That is, it makes no sense to assume that a firm that uses short-term debt will concurrently hold material cash or other short-term deposits (we ignore small balances, which the user can incorporate as constants within the IF statements). As a result, we have two "IF" statements that render one of these items zero while the other obtains a positive value that balances the BS. The specific equations of the BS and P&L are given in Exhibit 3.

Exhibit 2
Time-varying parameters

TIME-VARYING PARAMETERS	**Name**
Tax Rate	TAX_RATE
Contingent Dividend Payout %	DIV_RATE
Contingent LTD/Equity Ratio	LTD_EQ_RATIO
Receivables/Sales	REC_S
Inventories/Sales	INV_S
Payables/Sales	PAY_S
Depreciation Rate	DEPR_RATE
Credit Rate	CREDIT_RATE
Short Term Debt Rate	STD_RATE
Long Term Debt Rate	LTD_RATE
Average LTD Period	LTD_YRS

Let us describe the way our BS is computed: First note that Receivables (REC) and Inventories (INV) are calculated by multiplying sales of year t (as given in Table 3 of the budget) by the constant ratio as presented in Exhibit 2. Second, fixed assets at cost (ATCOST) are estimated based on Table 12 of the budget model and the level of ATCOST in the previous year. After subtracting accumulated depreciation

Exhibit 3 – Equations of Balance Sheet and Profit and Loss Statements

BALANCE SHEET

Name	Item	Equation at period *t* (subscript "*t*" omitted if all arguments refer to "*t*")	Comments
	ASSETS		
CASH	Cash & Bank Deposits	=IF(TLIABIL-(REC+INV+NFA)<0, 0, TLIABIL-(REC+INV+NFA))	If the value in this cell is negative, place zero, otherwise place the value
REC	Receivables	=SALES*REC_S	Calculated based on Exhibit 2 parameter
INV	Inventories	=SALES*INV_S	Calculated based on Exhibit 2 parameter
ATCOST	At cost	=TINVS_CF$_t$+ATCOST$_{t-1}$	The sum of investment in FA from the budget model at *t*, plus ATCOST at *t*-1
AC_DEPR	Accumulated Deprec.	=AC_DEPR$_{t-1}$+(ATCOST$_{t-1}$+ATCOST$_t$)/2*DEPR_RATE	This assumes that new fixed assets are purchased, on average, at mid-year
NFA	Net Fixed Assets	=ATCOST-AC_DEPR	
TASSETS	TOTAL ASSETS	=(CASH+REC+INV+NFA)	
	LIABILITIES		
STD	Short Term Debt	=IF((TASSETS-CASH-(AP+LTD+EQUITY+RET_ER))>0, TASSETS-CASH-(AP+LTD+EQUITY+RET_ER),0)	If TASSETS-CASH is higher than the sum of all other liabilities, use short-term debt, or zero otherwise.
AP	Accounts Payable	=SALES*PAY_S	Calculated based on Exhibit 2 parameter
LTD	Long-Term Debt	=IF((EQUITY+RET_ER)>0,LTD_Equity_Ratio*(EQUITY+RET_ER),0)	LTD can only be raised if (EQUITY+RET_ER)>0, and according to the LTD_Equity_Ratio.
EQUITY	Stock	=STOCK$_{t-1}$+EQUITY_RAISING$_t$	From Table B of Exhibit 4
RET_ER	Accumulated Retained Earnings	=RET_ER$_{t-1}$+RETAINED$_t$	From P&L statement
TLIABIL	TOTAL LIABILITIES	=STD+AP+LTD+EQUITY+RET_ER	

Exhibit 3 – Continued

PROFIT & LOSS STATEMENT

Name	Item	**Equation at period *t*** (subscript "*t*" omitted if all arguments refer to "*t*")	Comments
SALES	Sales	=TOTAL SALES	Reference to Table 3 of budget
COGS	Cost of Goods Sold (COGS)	=TOTAL VARIABLE COST (COGS)	Reference to Table 5 of budget
DIR_LAB	Direct Labor	=TOTAL DIRECT LABOR	Reference to Table 9 of budget
NOI	Net Operating Income	=SALES-COGS-DIR_LAB	
G&A&M	G&A and Marketing	=TOTAL DIRECT LABOR+TOTAL M&S+TOTAL G&A	References to Tables 9, 10, and 11 of budget
DEPREC	Depreciation	=AC_DEPR$_t$- AC_DEPR$_{t-1}$	
EBIT	EBIT	=NOI-G&A&M-DEPREC	
INTER	Net Interest Paid (Earned)	=LTD*LTD_RATE+STD*STD_RATE-CASH*CREDIT_RATE	Calculated based on Exhibit 2
PBT	Earnings Before Tax	=EBIT-INTER	
TAX	Tax Payments	=IF(ACC_PBT<0,0,TAX_RATE*MIN(ACC_PBT,PBT))	See explanation in the text
NET_PRO	Net Profit	=PBT-TAX	
DIV_PAY	Dividend Payout $	=IF(NET_PRO<0,0,NET_PRO*DIV_RATE)	
RETAINED	Retained Earnings	=NET_PRO-DIV_PAY	
Supplemental calculation			
ACC_PBT	Accumulated PBT	=IF(AND(ACC_PBT$_{t-1}$>0,PBT$_t$<0),NET_PRO$_t$,AC_PBT$_{t-1}$+PBT$_t$)	See explanation in the text

(AC_DEPR), one obtains net fixed assets (NFA)[4]. Our first plug number, CASH equals the difference between all financial resources (TLIABIL) and all uses (REC+INV+NFA). If the difference is negative, i.e., there is a need for more resources, the formula places zero in CASH, but if it is positive, the difference (i.e., excess resources), is classified as CASH.

On the liabilities side, accounts payable (AP) is calculated as a fraction of sales, representing average payment arrangements. Long-term debt (LTD) is calculated by multiplying the period-t parameter LTD_EQUITY_RATIO by the sum of equity capital (EQUITY+RET_ER), but only if this sum is positive. This represents an assumption that long-term debt will not be granted unless shareholders demonstrate their faith in the firm by making total equity positive (one can modify the equation and require a specific hurdle). The level of equity stock investment (EQUITY) is the sum of previous year balance plus current year equity raised. The latter is an input that the analyst plugs into Table 14 ¬(Financing Activities) as detailed in the Valuation section of the model below. Lastly, Accumulated Retained Earnings (RET_ER) is the sum of previous year RET_ER plus current year Retained Earnings (RETAINED), from the P&L.

This brings us to explain how the second plug number is calculated: Short Term Debt (STD) is calculated by applying an IF statement where we subtract all resources of funds on the liabilities side from total uses (other than cash) on the assets side (TASSETS-CASH-(AP+LTD+EQUITY+RET_ER)). If this difference is positive (i.e., there are more uses than resources of funds), then this difference implies a need for more short term debt (the difference enters into STD). If, however, this difference is negative, meaning there are more resources than uses, then there is no need to raise short-term debt, and STD becomes zero.

C. *The profit and loss statement*

Our P&L presents the firm's estimated profitability, but its accuracy and relevance depend on the consistency of data entered into the budget model and the

---

[4] It is assumed here that book values are consistent with market values of net fixed assets. This assumption is relevant for the case whenever the Modigliani and Miller (1958) approach is used to determine the discount rate.

firm's business plan. We highlight this linkage because it is a key in determining whether the pro forma analysis is informative. As noted, an important advantage of this model is that its underlying assumptions are verifiable across different aspects of the firm's operations.

The P&L starts with estimated sales (from Table 3), subtracts COGS (Table 5), and direct labor (Table 9) to yield net operating income (NOI)[5] . EBIT is obtained next by subtracting G&A and Marketing expenses (Tables 9, 10, 11) and current depreciation (the difference between AC_DEPRt-AC_DEPRt-1). The only remaining exogenous parameters are the tax rate (TAX_RATE), the contingent dividend payout (DIV_RATE), and the leverage policy (LTD_EQ_RATIO), as detailed in Exhibit 2.

The calculation of tax payments is somewhat more complex, as it accounts for loss carried forward, even in cases where a sequence of profitable years is interrupted by years of losses more than once (most models do not do that). The reason this attribute is important in our model is the fact that we do not assume an exogenous growth rate for sales. Absent this assumption, profitability might not increase monotonically. To implement this attribute we calculate Accumulated Profit Before Tax (ACC_PBT), in the following manner on the Excel spreadsheet:

```
=IF(AND(ACC_PBTt-1>0, PBTt<0), NET_PROt, AC_PBTt-1+PBTt)        (1)
```

As long as the firm is profitable, or started with losses but continues with gains, this formula accumulates gains from one year to the next (the right-most term, AC_PBTt-1+PBTt). However, in order to reset the ACC_PBT calculator, this statement requires that two conditions be met: First, that ACC_PBTt-1 is strictly positive, and second, that PBTt is strictly negative. Jointly these conditions imply that the firm changed phases from profits to losses. If this occurs, the current loss, NET_PROt, replaces the value of ACC_PBTt, and this calculator starts accumulating losses. If future years are profitable, current profits will be added to the accumulated losses, until none remains (i.e., loss carried forward fully). However, this poses a problem in the first year of gains (after a series of losses), because the firm should be taxed on the lowest between current-year profits and ACC_PBT, net of any loss carried

---

[5] From a pure accounting perspective, our measure of NOI should actually be denoted "contribution margin", because it does not include variable marketing cost.

forward. To incorporate that we devised this formula in the Tax Payment (TAX) calculation:

=IF(ACC_PBT<0,0,TAX_RATE*MIN(ACC_PBT,PBT)) (2)

This statement implies that if ACC_PBT is negative, the firm needs not pay any taxes (TAX becomes zero). But otherwise, the firm's tax payment is the product of the TAX_RATE times the minimum between ACC_PBT or PBT. For example, if the firm earned a $100 PBT this year, but ACC_PBT is $80 (because it carried a loss of $20 from previous year), it will pay taxes on $80, not $100.

Finally, note that as in all worksheet-based models of financial statements, Retained Earnings (RETAINED) from the P&L enters into Accumulated Retained Earnings (RET_ER) in the BS. This changes the ratio of long-term-debt to equity and the entire level of the BS, therefore changing short-term debt, cash, and interest payments, which in turn change the P&L in a circular way.[6] While circular reference models will not necessarily converge to a stable solution, the way our model is structured assures convergence.

IV. Valuation model

To determine the firm's value we discount two elements separately. First we discount the period Free Cash Flow (FCF), normally spanning over the periods 0,1,...,5. The limit at period 5 is warranted if longer detailed projections become less informative due to increasing uncertainty. If the simulated pro forma is conducted for mature and stable firms like hotels, or utilities, the projection can be extended as necessary (in the Excel model this means copying the last column rightward). If possible, the last year, period 5, should reflect a steady-state year. The second element of the valuation model is made of the expected terminal value of the firm, discounted to the present. We provide three alternative valuation approaches to the terminal value and calculate a weighted average.

The valuation model obtains most of its data from the P&L and BS statements. It is comprised of the equations detailed in Exhibit 4. Table A of Exhibit 4 constitutes

---

[6] When applying the model on an Excel worksheet the user should make sure the worksheet is set to accommodate iterative calculations.

the standard transformation of net profit or loss, from the P&L statement to FCF, before financing activities (Brealey, Myers, and Marcus, 2009, Fletcher and Ulrich, 2010). Table B lists the cash flow implications of financing activities. Because the amount of equity raised is a managerial decision, the analyst may plug in different values until the cash-flow implications are satisfactory, primarily with respect to Accumulated Balance, at the bottom row of Table B. If the amount raised by issuing equity shares is too little, the firm will be forced to use Short-Term Debt, while rendering Cash to be zero. Clearly, management would normally prefer to raise sufficient equity capital such that Accumulated Balances throughout the periods are deemed "sufficient". The level of sufficient balances depends on the level of uncertainty in the firm's expected cash flows.

An additional item deserving a brief explanation is the calculation of LTD Principal Repayment (row k in Exhibit 4). We use the Excel formula PPMT, which requires, as the second input parameter, the current period of the loan. For lack of a better default, we add one to the first period of the pro forma analysis (typically 0, denoted PERIOD). The reason for adding one is that Excel will not calculate the principal repayment if the value in this entry is lower than one. The practical implication is that this calculation implicitly assumes that the loan was taken on the first day of the first period.

Table C accommodates an analyst's estimate of the risk-adjusted discount rate for the firm, which may vary across years. This parameter may be estimated by the CAPM Beta, by using comparable firms' cost of equity capital, or by other means. We note that the user should not use the Weighted Average Cost of Capital (WACC) of Modigliani and Miller (1958) in the case of a new technology firm. The reason is that the derivation of the WACC assumes stationary cash flows. Because this model applies to both new technology ventures (which, by definition, do not resemble the riskiness of existing technologies) and to existing technologies, we let the user determine the appropriate discount rate. Nevertheless, should the user conclude that WACC is applicable, then the capital structure of the firm must be accounted for, as leverage changes over time. In this case the cost of equity capital within the WACC changes with leverage.

Because the discount rate may vary throughout the estimation period, the cash flow of period T must be discounted by the product of all discount rates preceding T.

Formally, the present value of the cash flow at T may be expressed as:

$$PV(CF_T) = \frac{CF_T}{\prod_{t=0}^{T}(1+k_t)} \tag{3}$$

Table C concludes by discounting each of the cash flows by the appropriate discount rates ( ). By summing the discounted cash flows, one obtains the net present value of this venture, for the periods 0 – T.

The last remaining step in the valuation section is estimating the terminal value of the firm, as if it were sold or liquidated on the first day after the last pro forma period (T) has ended. Table A of Exhibit 5 presents three alternative ways to estimate the terminal value of the firm. First is a multiplier of free cash flow. It is assumed that the FCF of the last period ($2,401 in period 5 of our example) represents a typical year of the FCF, and it is multiplied by an industry-relevant multiplier. We assume here that the multiplier is 4.5, therefore the period-5 amount is $10,802. Using equation (3), the present value of this amount is $3,540. The second alternative is based on the dividend growth model, where the period-5 cash flow, assumed to grow to infinity at a constant rate, g, is discounted by the period-5 discount rate (representing the long-term discount rate). This valuation method amounts to $10,936 in period 5 and, after discounting by (3), its present value is $3,583. Third is the multiplier based on net profit, here taken as 5.0. It yields a $12,479 terminal valuation with a discounted value of $4,089. This method will be less meaningful if the firm is losing, therefore its weighted value in the overall assessment of terminal value assessment will be lower than the other two methods.

In a steady-state firm, the three estimation techniques should not diverge from one another materially. In technology firms, however, periods 0 – T might yield negative profits, rendering methods A and C less informative, while future growth opportunities will be more reliably estimated by using the growth model of method B. If the PV of the terminal values greatly exceed the NPV of periods 0 – 5 cash flows, this implies that the profit opportunities the venture offers are primarily long-term, an aspect that increases the risks for shareholders, and therefore higher discount rates are required. An appropriate representation of the risks involved (i.e., increasing the cost of capital), would reduce the PV of terminal value. Unfortunately, there is no prescription for the "proper" interactions and balance between these arguments.

Exhibit 4
Valuation model of the firm at the end of period *t*

	A. FREE CASH FLOW ($,000)	
		Equation at period *t* (subscript "*t*" omitted if all arguments refer to "*t*")
a	Net Profit	=NET_PRO
b	Add Back Depreciation	=DEPREC
c	Less Increase in Inventories	$=-(INV_t-INV_{t-1})$
d	Less Increase in Receivables	$=-(REC_t-REC_{t-1})$
e	Add Increase in Payables	$=AP_t-AP_{t-1}$
f	Cash-Flow from Operating Activities	=a+b+c+d+e
g	Less Increase in Fixed Assets At-Cost	$=-(ATCOST_t-ATCOST_{t-1})$
h	FCF before Financing Activities	=f+g

	B. FINANCING ACTIVITIES	
i	Equity Raising	Input data
j	Change in Loans (LTD+STD)	$=(STD_t+LTD_t)-(STD_{t-1}+LTD_{t-1})$
k	LTD Principal Repayment	=PPMT(LTD_RATE, PERIOD+1, LTD_YRS, LTD)
l	Dividend Payment	=-DIV_PAY
m	Total Resources	=i+j+k+l
n	Periodic Balance	=h+m
o	Accumulated Balance	$=o_{t-1}+n_t$

	C. PV OF FCF (PERIODS 0-6)	
p	Risk Adjusted Discount Rate	Input data
q	Discount Factor	$=(1+q_{t-1})*(1+p_t)$
r	Annual Cash Flow PV	$=h_t/q_t$
s	Cash Flow NPV	$=SUM(r_0+r_1+r_2+\ldots+r_5)$

Exhibit 5
Estimating terminal value

A. PV OF TERMINAL VALUE	0	1	2	3	4	5
Terminal Value Method A:						
CF_5*Multiplier(CF):	m(CF)=	*4.5*				10,802
Terminal Value (A) PV	**3,540**					
Terminal Value Method B:						
CF_5*(1+g)/(k-g):	g=	*2.5%*				10,936
Terminal Value (B) PV	**3,583**					
Terminal Value Method C:						
Net-Profits$_5$*Multiplier(NP):	m(NP)=	*5.0*				12,479
Terminal Value (C) PV	**4,089**					

B. Total Company Value	Method A	Method B	Method C
Cash Flow NPV	1,875	1,875	1,875
Terminal Value	3,540	3,583	4,089
Total Company Value	**5,415**	**5,458**	**5,964**
Subjective Method Weights	*25%*	*40%*	35%
Weighted Value NPV:	**5,624**		

Note: Input data cells in italics.

Lastly, Table B assigns weights of relevance that the analyst places on each of the three ways the terminal value is calculated, according to his or her belief of the more relevant valuation method. The analyst than adds the NPV of periods 0 – 5 FCF, and by simple multiplication obtains the weighted average overall value of the venture. Based on the financial information this model yields, the analyst can conduct sensitivity analyses, what-if scenarios, and calculate financial ratios to examine the robustness of the results.[7]

[7] To illustrate the rather moderate impact that exogenous parameters have on the firm's value, consider the case where the ratio of inventories/sales (INV_S), which at a benchmark model was 15%, obtains values of 10% (20%), as INV_S declines (increases), respectively. Such variations of ±33% in the benchmark parameter increase (reduce) the firm's valuation by about 7.2% to the relevant direction. Similar results are obtained when altering receivables to sales or payables to sales.

V. Summary and Conclusions

This paper presents a pro forma financial statements model that builds on a detailed business plan, where the latter's key operational implications are represented in a budget. By so doing, the model replaces most of the constant ratios to sales that most pro forma models assume as exogenous parameters. Should the analyst use the budget to reflect the firm's operational activities as prescribed by the business plan, the resulting pro forma statements would reflect the firm's prospects rather accurately. The reason is that once the budget feeds the financial statements, the remaining exogenous parameters have little effect on the key measures of performance. As a result, our valuation model, which transforms the net income into cash flow and adds terminal value, obtains robust results that the analyst can justify based on operational aspects. This makes the model highly relevant for the valuation of early stage, new technology ventures, as well as mature and stable firms.

REFERENCES

Arnold, Tom, and Jerry James, 2000. "Finding firm value without a Pro Forma Analysis", Financial Analysts Journal, 56(2) 77-84.

Benninga, Simon, and Oded Sarig. 1997. "Corporate Finance: A Valuation Approach". New York: McGraw-Hill.

Brealey, Richard A., Myers, Stewart C., & Marcus, Allen J. 2009. "Fundamentals of corporate finance" (6th Ed.). New York: McGraw-Hill/Irwin.

Copeland, T., T. Koller, and J. Murrin. 1994. "Valuation: Measuring and managing the value of companies", 2nd ed. New York: John Wiley & Sons.

Core, John E., Wayne R. Guay, and Andrew Van Buskirk. 2003. "Market valuations in the New Economy: an investigation of what has changed". Journal of Accounting and Economics, 34(1-3): 43-67.

Fletcher, Harold, and Thomas Ulrich, 2010. "The statement of cash flows using financial statement equations", Business Education & Accreditation, 2(1), 15-26.

Modigliani, Franco and Merton H. Miller. (1958). "The cost of capital, corporation finance and the theory of investment". American Economic Review 48: 261-297.

Schwartz, Eduardo S. and Mark Moon. 2000. "Rational Pricing of Internet Companies" Financial Analysts Journal, 56(3): 62-75.

Schwartz, Eduardo S. and Mark Moon. 2001. "Rational Pricing of Internet Companies Revisited". Financial Review, 36(4): 7-26.

Trueman, Brett, M. H. Franco Wong, and Xiao-Jun Zhang. 2000. "The eyeballs have it: Searching for the value in internet stocks". Journal of Accounting Research, 38(3): 137-162.

THE JOURNAL OF ENTREPRENEURIAL FINANCE VOL. 16, NO. 2 (SPRING 2013) 75-96

SB IPOs and IPO Anomalies: An Empirical Analysis of the Small Firm Uniqueness Hypothesis

James C. Brau[1]
Brigham Young University

J. Troy Carpenter[2]
Brigham Young University

ABSTRACT

The purpose of this paper is to provide a direct test of the small-firm uniqueness hypothesis advanced by Ang (1991). We do this by using the SB-IPO program of the SEC as our instrument to define a small firm. Having identified small firms, we test the three IPO anomalies to see if small firms differ from large firms along these dimensions. We find that SB IPOs experience the three anomalies; however, they do so in disparate ways than mainline IPOs do. In sum, we provide support for the small firm uniqueness hypothesis.

JEL Classification: G24, G28, G38
Key words: IPO, Initial Public Offering, Anomalies, Small Firm Uniqueness, SB-2

I. INTRODUCTION

PRIOR STUDIES OF MAINLINE IPOS have demonstrated consistently that IPOs exhibit three primary "anomalies." First, in seminal papers, Logue (1973) and Ibbotson (1975) document that IPOs are underpriced on average. That is, the closing price soon after

---

[1] James C. Brau, Professor of Finance, Brigham Young University Tel. 801.318.7919, Fax. 267.654.5268, jbrau@byu.edu
[2] J. Troy Carpenter, Research Associate and Computing Analyst, Brigham Young University, Tel. 801.422.3166, Fax. 801.422.0741, troy.carpenter@byu.edu

ISSN: 1551-9570

the IPO is significantly higher than the issue price for large samples over long periods of time. Second, Ritter (1991) and Loughran and Ritter (1995) documented the long-run underperformance of mainline IPOs based on risk-adjusted benchmarks. Third, Ibbotson and Jaffe (1975) and Ritter (1984) showed the existence of hot IPO markets based on underpricing and volume of issuance.

The purpose of our paper is to empirically test if these anomalies are robust to small firms. Our instrument for a small firm is a firm that chooses to file for its IPO using the SB-2 program (instead of the mainline S-1 program).[3] Our research question is of interest because extant literature argues that small businesses are unique (e.g., Ang, 1991; Timmons and Spinelli, 2007). By empirically examining the three IPO anomalies in SB-2 IPOs vis-à-vis S-1 IPOs, it is possible to explicitly test the small-business uniqueness hypothesis.

In the aggregate, we find support for the small-firm uniqueness hypothesis—small firms are different from large firms along many dimensions (Ang, 1991). We find that SB-2 IPOs differ along many dimensions from S-1 IPOs. For example, SB-2 IPOs tend to have less-prestigious auditors and underwriters. Finally, we demonstrate that while SB-2 IPOs appear to possess the same IPO anomalies that have been previously documented in the mainstream IPO literature, they do so in differing degrees. Surprisingly, SB-2 IPOs experience lower underpricing and at least as good long-run market-adjusted performance.

The remainder of the paper proceeds as follows. In the next section we develop the theoretical predictions driven from a review of the literature. The empirical work is detailed in the next section, consisting of Data, Empirical Methods, and Results. The final section concludes.

[3] A much lesser-known path to an IPO, designed specifically for small businesses is to file form SB-2 with the Securities and Exchange Commission (SEC). The 1992 SB-2 legislation was enacted for the specific purpose of giving small firms less restricted access to US capital markets by reducing the burden for registration and reporting. For a firm to qualify to use the SB-2 form it must be located in either the US or Canada and had less than $25 million in revenues in the last fiscal year. It also must have less than $25 million in public float.

II. LITERATURE REVIEW, THEORETICAL DEVELOPMENT, AND TESTABLE HYPOTHESES

The convergence of the small firm uniqueness hypothesis and entrepreneurial finance has not received much academic attention. We have found five papers that have at least partially tested what we examine in this paper. The research of Brau and Osteryoung (2001) and Brau and Gee (2010) both study micro-IPOs while Bradley, Cooney, Dolvin, and Jordan (2006) study penny-stock IPOs. These studies implicitly examine the small firm-uniqueness hypothesis, although they do not explicitly state this is what they are doing. Brau and Carpenter (2012a,b) study SB-2 IPOs as a proxy for small firms. In this paper, we employ the same data as Brau and Carpenter (2012a,b) but ask fundamentally different questions.

Brau and Osteryoung (2001) study SCOR prospectus companies. In the early 1980s, the Reagan administration initiated policies to remove regulatory burdens from small businesses in an attempt to make acquiring capital less costly (i.e., same intent as the SB-2 program). Brau and Osteryoung (2001) examine marketing mechanisms, expenses, ownership, governance, offering characteristics, business life stage, and signaling variables for 73 SCORs from the state of Washington. They find the number of directors, size of the largest block, and early-stage offers all impact the success of a SCOR offering.

Because SCORs do not have publicly-traded stock prices, Brau and Osteryoung (2001) define a successful offering as a firm that raised enough capital to break escrow. The limitations of non-public stock prices and unaudited financial statements prohibit the testing of the three IPO anomalies with the SCOR sample, and make the comparison with mainline IPOs very difficult. As a result, Brau and Osteryoung (2001) are not able to perform these tests. Our use of an SB-2 sample expands the research of small firm uniqueness by allowing us to perform this type of testing. In a follow-up study, Brau and Gee (2010) expand the study of SCORs to a national database.

In contrast to SCORs, Bradley et al. (2006) study publicly-traded penny stocks and, as such, can examine the traditional IPO anomalies and can compare penny-stock IPOs with mainline IPOs. Bradley et al. (2006) define a penny-stock IPO as:

> ". . . an issue that meets the following three criteria: 1) is not issued by an investment advisor (e.g., not a closed-end fund), 2) its offer price is $5 or less, and 3) is not listed on a national exchange or market . . . . Thus, we classify IPOs listed on the NYSE, AMEX, or Nasdaq National

> Market as 'ordinary' without regard to their offer prices. IPOs listed on other markets (such as the Nasdaq SmallCap Market, OTC Bulletin Board, pink sheets or regional exchanges) are classified as penny stocks if the offering is not issued by an investment advisor and the offer price is \$5 or less."

By using this definition, Bradley et al. (2006) are able to examine the mainline (what they call "ordinary") IPO issues of initial returns (i.e., underpricing), long-run performance, lockup lengths, and underwriting gross spreads. The extant mainline IPO literature demonstrates that IPOs are consistently, on average, underpriced (e.g., see the seminal work of Logue (1973) and Ibbotson (1975)). Underpricing, as defined by this literature, is typically the first-day return of the stock. As for IPO long-run performance, many studies of mainline IPOs (e.g., Ritter (1991) and Loughran and Ritter (1995)) show that IPOs underperform on a risk-adjusted basis. Pertaining to lockup lengths, Field and Hanka (2001) show that lockup lengths for mainline IPOs have clustered on 180 days. Finally, Chen and Ritter (2000) document that underwriter spreads have clustered at 7% for mainline IPOs.

Bradley et al. (2006) find significant differences between penny-stock and non-penny-stock IPOs. For the period 1990–1998, penny-stock IPOs have higher underpricing, lower long-run stock returns, longer lockups, and larger gross spreads. Specifically, penny-stock IPOs experience an average underpricing of 22.4%, significantly greater than ordinary IPOs (15.4%) at a *p*-value of 0.0003. The three-year (five-year) market-adjusted returns for penny-stock IPOs is -101.8% (-126.4%) contrasted with -39.9% (-55.2%) for ordinary IPOs (both *p*-values <0.01). As for lockups, the average length of the 207 penny-stock IPOs with data is 452 days, compared to 180 days for ordinary IPOs. Finally, penny-stock IPOs group around a standard underwriter spread of 10%, whereas ordinary IPOs group at 7%.

In addition, the authors find penny-stock IPOs offered by underwriters who have undergone SEC enforcement actions have even higher underpricing (31.6%) and worse long-run returns (3-year = -131.8%, 5-year = -162.6%). Bradley et al. (2006) do not examine the issue of registration type (S-1 vs. SB-2). We believe our tests of the SB-2 program to be the first.

The mainline IPO literature has documented three traditional IPO anomalies: underpricing, long-run performance, and hot markets. In this section, we test to determine if these anomalies exist for SB-2 IPOs in an absolute and relative (i.e., to S-1

IPOs) framework. Continuing the purpose of testing SB-2 IPO quality vis-à-vis S-1 IPO quality, we test the following four hypotheses:

> *H1: SB-2 IPOs have significant, positive first-day underpricing which is higher than S-1 IPOs.*
> *H2: SB-2 IPOs have significant, negative long-run stock price performance which is worse than S-1 IPOs.*
> *H3: SB-2 IPOs delist for negative reasons more frequently than S-1 IPOs.*
> *H4: SB-2 IPOs have significant market cycles which are more volatile than S-1 IPOs.*

The data for underpricing, long-run returns, and delisting are taken from CRSP's daily stock return files. Frequency of IPO issuance is taken from SDC. Beatty and Ritter (1986) argue and demonstrate in a seminal empirical paper on underpricing that firms with greater uncertainty have higher underpricing. If SB-2s are riskier (i.e., lower quality) than S-1 IPOs, we expect H1 to hold. Beginning with Ritter (1991) the long-run stock performance of IPOs has been shown to be subpar, typically underperforming risk-adjusted or market benchmarks. If SB-2 IPOs are of lower quality (and if they are priced inefficiently at offering and by the initial market prices) then H2 follows. The delisting measure, H3, taken from Brau, Brown, and Osteryoung (2004), is an additional proxy for long-run outcome/performance. H4 is designed to test the hot market anomaly (e.g., Ritter, 1984).

III. EMPIRICAL WORK

A. Data

We employ the same data and methods used by Brau and Carpenter (2012a) who distinguish small firms as those that filed an IPO using the SB-2 form, and compare them to similar-sized companies that issued an IPO with the standard S-1 form.

Just as Brau and Carpenter (2012a), we begin with an initial sample of SB-2 and S-1 IPOs taken from the SDC's New Issues database issued between 1993 and 2007 (1993 was the first year with reliable SB-2 data and 2007 was the last year when an SB-2 IPO was filed) and combine this with return and financial data from the CRSP and Compustat datasets. We calculate abnormal returns (defined subsequently) from the CRSP data and gather pre-IPO revenues from the Compustat data. After removing all firms with more than $25 million in sales and excluding all financial firms we are also left with 1,899 IPOs in our final sample with 1,356 S-1 IPOs and 543 SB-2 IPOs.[4] Tables I and II report the frequency distributions for the sample parsed on issue year and industry, respectively.

B. *Empirical Methods and Results*

We define *Initial Return* (short-term), our proxy for IPO underpricing, as the first-day return from offer price to closing price (Bradley et al. (2006)). The *One-Year Abnormal Return* (long-term) is the cumulative raw return, adjusted for the CRSP all-index value-weighted cumulative return (Loughran and Ritter (1995)). Table IV reports the descriptive statistics as well as difference tests for these variables. Compared to the S-1 pooled sample, SB-2 IPOs have an average (median) *Initial Return* of 15% (8%) while S-1 IPOs have an average (median) of nearly 37% (13%). The difference in means (medians) – 22% (-5%) is significant with a *p*-value of 0.0001 (0.0001).[5] The pair-matched results are very similar to these pooled results.

Using pooled data, the S-1 IPO *One-Year Abnormal Return* average (median) is -9.9% (-35%) compared to the SB-2 average (median) of -17.0% (-33.5%). The difference in means (-7.2%) is significant (p = 0.0845); however, the difference in medians (1.5%) is not significant (p = 0.8642). The pair-matched benchmark sample is not consistent with the pool-matched sample in this instance. Using pair-matched firms, SB-2 IPOs outperform S-1 IPOs in the mean (2.2%, p = 0.6631) and in the median (9.2%, p = 0.0062). Because of this inconsistency, we will rely on the subsequent ordinary least square (OLS) and two stage least square (2SLS) multivariate results before interpreting the long-run results.

In sum, using univariate analysis, H1 is rejected because SB-2 IPOs have *significantly less underpricing* than S-1 IPOs, contrary to predictions. The results for H2, long-run returns, are mixed.

---

[4] We follow the same methods as Brau and Carpenter (2012a). See their data section for a detailed description of data collection.

[5] For a review of the IPO underpricing literature see Daily et al. (2003).

Table I. Sample Frequencies by Issue Year

Panel A: S-1 IPOs

Issue Year	Pooled Sample Frequency	Pooled Sample Percent	Pair-Matched Sample Frequency	Pair-Matched Sample Percent
1993	123	9.1	67	12.3
1994	106	7.8	45	8.3
1995	119	8.8	47	8.7
1996	201	14.8	71	13.1
1997	122	9.0	54	9.9
1998	72	5.3	30	5.5
1999	245	18.1	105	19.3
2000	205	15.1	79	14.6
2001	18	1.3	4	0.7
2002	5	0.4	2	0.4
2003	7	0.5	2	0.4
2004	40	3.0	12	2.2
2005	25	1.8	8	1.5
2006	30	2.2	4	0.7
2007	34	2.5	12	2.2
2008-11	4	0.3	1	0.2

Panel B: SB-2 IPOs

Issue Year	Frequency	Percent	Cumulative Frequency	Cumulative Percent
1993	82	15.1	82	15.1
1994	83	15.3	165	30.4
1995	100	18.4	265	48.8
1996	128	23.6	393	72.4
1997	64	11.8	457	84.2
1998	31	5.7	488	89.9
1999	15	2.8	503	92.6
2000	10	1.8	513	94.5
2001	4	0.7	517	95.2
2002	3	0.6	520	95.8
2003	4	0.7	524	96.5
2004	6	1.1	530	97.6
2005	2	0.4	532	98.0
2006	6	1.1	538	99.1
2007	5	0.9	543	100
2008-11	0	0.0	543	100

Table II. Sample Frequencies by Industry Group

Panel A: S-1 IPOs				
	Pooled Sample		Pair-Matched Sample	
Industry	Frequency	Percent	Frequency	Percent
A	1	0.1	1	0.2
B	30	2.2	4	0.7
C	6	0.4	6	1.1
D	574	42.3	247	45.5
E	87	6.4	22	4.1
F	16	1.2	25	4.6
G	46	3.4	37	6.8
I	588	43.4	194	35.7
Missing	8	0.6	7	1.3

Panel B: SB-2 IPOs				
			Cumulative	Cumulative
Industry	Frequency	Percent	Frequency	Percent
A	1	0.18	1	0.2
B	4	0.74	5	0.9
C	6	1.1	11	2.0
D	247	45.49	258	47.5
E	22	4.05	280	51.6
F	25	4.6	305	56.2
G	37	6.81	342	63.0
I	194	35.73	536	98.7
Missing	7	1.29	543	100

Industry description	SIC Manual Division	Two-Digit Major Group
Agriculture, Forestry, and Fishing	A	01–09
Mining	B	10–14
Construction	C	15–17
Manufacturing	D	20–39
Transportation, Communications, Electric, Gas, and Sanitary Services	E	40–49
Wholesale Trade	F	50–51
Retail Trade	G	52–59
Finance, Insurance, and Real Estate	H	60–67
Services	I	70–89
Public Administration	J	91–97

Table III. Logit Model of SB-2 Versus S-1.
Dependent variable SB = 1 or SB = 0.

	Pooled		Pair-Matched	
	Estimate	*p*-value	Estimate	*p*-value
Intercept	1.97	0.0031	2.45	0.0022
Big Six	-1.02	0.0006	-1.22	0.0013
UW Rank	0.83	0.8524	-0.45	0.9293
log(Sales)	0.18	0.1472	0.62	<.0001
Cash Flow	0.03	0.4311	0.01	0.7914
Exchange	-0.72	0.0071	-0.87	0.0061
ROA	-0.03	0.5912	-0.04	0.5544
log(Age)	-0.04	0.7558	-0.15	0.3455
VC	-0.13	0.5260	-0.08	0.7680
Debt/Assets	0.01	0.8902	0.02	0.8853
Delaware Corp	-0.41	0.0313	-0.25	0.2864
Offer Size	-0.18	<.0001	-0.16	<.0001
Internet IPO	1.43	0.0047	1.67	0.0062
Dual Share Class	-0.31	0.6377	-0.63	0.4040
Lockup Length	0.005	<.0001	0.005	<.0001
Years	Yes		Yes	
Industry	Yes		Yes	
Psuedo R^2	65.1%		66.1%	

In order to more fully test *Initial Return* and *One-Year Abnormal Return* we estimate OLS and 2SLS regression models. Table V reports the results for *Initial Return* using the following OLS model:

$$\textit{Initial Return} = \beta_1 SB + \beta_2 \textit{Big Six} + \beta_3 \textit{UWRank} + \beta_4 \textit{log(Sales)} + \beta_5 \textit{Cash Flow} + \beta_6 \textit{Exchange} + \beta_7 \textit{Overhang} + \beta_8 \textit{log(Age)} + \beta_9 VC + \beta_{10} \textit{Debt/Assets} + \beta_{11} \textit{Delaware Corp} + \beta_{12} \textit{Internet IPO} + \beta_{13} \textit{Dual Share Class} + \beta_{14} \textit{Lockup Length} + \beta_{(years)} \textit{Years}_{(1993\text{-}2007)} + \beta_{(industries)} \textit{Industry}_{1(A\text{-}I)} + \varepsilon. \quad (1)$$

Table IV. Descriptive Statistics and Difference Tests of After-Market Returns

Panel A. SB-2 IPOs				
Variable	Mean	Median		
Initial Return	15.0%	8.0%		
1-Year Return	-17.0%	-33.5%		
Panel B. S-1 IPOs				
	Pooled		Pair-Matched	
Variable	Mean	Median	Mean	Median
Initial Return	36.9%	13.0%	36.8%	12.5%
1-Year Return	-9.9%	-35.0%	-19.2%	-42.7%
Panel C. Differences (SB-2 minus S-1)				
	Pooled		Pair-Matched	
Variable	Mean	Median	Mean	Median
Initial Return	-21.9%	-5.0%	-21.8%	-4.5%
	(<.0001)	(<.0001)	(<.0001)	(<.0001)
1-Year Return	-7.2%	1.5%	2.2%	9.2%
	(0.0845)	(0.8642)	(0.6631)	(0.0062)

These variables are all defined in Appendix A. Bruton, Chahine, and Filatotchev (2009) show that owner retention significantly impacts entrepreneurial IPO underpricing. As such, we use *Overhang*, defined as shares retained divided by primary shares sold (Bradley and Jordan (2002)).

We estimate a two-stage model where the first stage contains a logit model modeling the choice of SB-2 or S-1. Several of the independent variables, as shown in Table III are significant including *Big Six, log(Sales), Exchange, Delaware Corp, Offersize, Internet IPO, and Lockup Length.* The purpose however, of the logit model is to estimate an *SB-hat* and then use it for the SB proxy variable in the OLS model with *Initial Return* as the dependent variable. As such, we will leave the inspection of Table III to the interested reader.

The primary variable of interest in Table V, Panel A is *SB*. The results indicate that we reject H1; SB-2s do not significantly under- or over-perform S-1 IPOs in the initial return. The OLS results seem to contradict the univariate results. However, Panel B, which removes the endogeneity of the SB-1 variable by using *SB-hat,* reports that in the pooled (pair-matched) benchmark sample, SB-2 IPOs have 2% (4%) less underpricing, both significant with *p*-values less than 0.0001. Thus, our univariate results are confirmed.

Table VI reports the results for the following model which tests H2, first using OLS with *SB* (Panel A) and then using 2SLS with *SB-hat* (Panel B):

$$\begin{aligned}&\textit{One-Year Abnormal Return} = \\ &\beta_1 SB + \beta_2 \textit{Underprice} + \beta_3 \textit{Big Six} + \beta_4 \textit{UW Rank} + \beta_5 \textit{log(Sales)} + \beta_6 \textit{Cash} \\ &\textit{Flow} + \beta_7 \textit{Exchange} + \beta_8 \textit{ROA} + \beta_9 \textit{log(Age)} + \beta_{10} \textit{VC} + \beta_{11} \textit{Debt/Assets} + \\ &\beta_{12} \textit{Delaware Corp} + \beta_{13} \textit{Internet IPO} + \beta_{14} \textit{Dual Share Class} + \beta_{15} \textit{Lockup} \\ &\textit{Length} + \beta_{16} \textit{Book/Market} + \beta_{(years)} \textit{Years}_{(1993\text{-}2007)} + \beta_{(industries)} \textit{Industry}_{1(A\text{-}I)} + \varepsilon. \qquad (2)\end{aligned}$$

All of these variables are defined previously, except for *Book/Market* equity, and *Underprice*. We add *Book/Market* following Barber and Lyon (1997) who show it is an important factor in explaining long-run IPO returns. *Underprice*, as defined above, is the first closing price divided by the offer price. In the 2SLS model, we also construct an *Underprice-hat* variable using the model in Equation 3. We include *Underprice* and *Underprice-hat* based on McConaughy, Dhatt, and Kim (1995) who argue that poor long-run IPO performance is due to investors who overpay.

The results in Table VI indicate that *SB* or *SB-hat* is only significant in the pair-matched 2SLS model (Panel B, last two columns). In general, the four models in Table VI indicate that SB-2 IPOs do not underperform S-1 IPOs over one year, and may even outperform them by 3%. Thus, we reject H2.

Table VII reports the frequency and various reasons that the companies in our sample were delisted. The statistics are for the first five years of a firm's life, so we include the IPOs in our sample from 1993 to 2004, which is 97.6% of the SB-2 sample, 93.2% of the pooled sample and 95.4% of the pair-matched sample. We do not include the later years of the sample because they do not have five years of life to

Table V. OLS and 2SLS Models of Underpricing

	Panel A. OLS Model: Initial Return				Panel B. 2SLS Model: Initial Return			
	Pooled		Pair-Matched		Pooled		Pair-Matched	
	Estimate	*p*-value	Estimate	*p*-value	Estimate	*p*-value	Estimate	*p*-value
SB or SB-hat	-0.04	0.2342	-0.06	0.1638	-0.02	<.0001	-0.04	<.0001
Big Six	-0.05	0.2066	-0.07	0.1706	-0.07	0.0745	-0.12	0.0131
UW Rank	1.66	<.0001	1.84	0.0033	1.25	0.0005	1.15	0.0688
log(Sales)	0.02	0.233	0.02	0.3377	0.02	0.2525	0.02	0.2362
Cash Flow	0.002	0.4537	-0.0003	0.9497	0.005	0.0556	0.01	0.22
Exchange	-0.002	0.9669	0.01	0.8934	-0.02	0.5268	-0.04	0.3906
Overhang	0.04	<.0001	0.05	<.0001	0.04	<.0001	0.05	<.0001
log(Age)	0.004	0.8093	0.01	0.6035	0.01	0.6708	0.02	0.3636
VC	-0.004	0.89	-0.004	0.9224	0.004	0.8754	-0.0001	0.9976
Debt/Assets	-0.01	0.2371	-0.01	0.3962	-0.01	0.2328	-0.01	0.319
Delaware Corp	0.04	0.1483	0.03	0.4024	0.03	0.2527	0.02	0.6224
Internet IPO	0.23	<.0001	0.32	<.0001	0.25	<.0001	0.36	<.0001
Dual Share Class	0.01	0.9052	-0.07	0.5003	-0.02	0.7469	-0.11	0.297
Lockup length	0.0003	0.0056	0.0003	0.0218	0.0003	0.0004	0.0004	0.0007
Intercept	0.20	0.014	0.12	0.2864	0.14	0.0791	0.09	0.3951
Years	Yes		Yes		Yes		Yes	
Industry	Yes		Yes		Yes		Yes	
Adj R^2	17.2%	<.0001	13.3%	<.0001	18.6%	<.0001	15.6%	<.0001

Table VI. OLS and 2SLS Models of 1-Year Abnormal Return

	Panel A. OLS Model: 1-Year Return				Panel B. 2SLS Model: 1-Year Return			
	Pooled		Pair-Matched		Pooled		Pair-Matched	
	Estimate	*p*-value	Estimate	*p*-value	Estimate	*p*-value	Estimate	*p*-value
SB or SB-hat	0.04	0.5709	0.09	0.1619	-0.0003	0.9665	0.03	0.0278
Underprice or Underprice-hat	-0.13	0.0138	-0.13	0.0157	0.39	0.2637	0.02	0.9516
Big Six	0.03	0.6456	-0.03	0.7317	0.05	0.5406	0.01	0.8893
UW Rank	1.08	0.1069	2.67	0.0037	-0.003	0.9974	2.72	0.0161
log(Sales)	0.03	0.3368	0.04	0.2785	0.01	0.6661	0.03	0.3753
Cash Flow	0.01	0.0359	0.01	0.0952	0.01	0.0461	0.01	0.2841
Exchange	0.11	0.1346	0.13	0.0536	0.09	0.1909	0.16	0.029
ROA	0.02	0.154	0.01	0.4062	0.02	0.1434	0.01	0.3557
log(Age)	-0.02	0.5153	-0.03	0.3257	-0.02	0.5918	-0.04	0.2496
VC	0.04	0.4165	-0.06	0.3165	0.03	0.5226	-0.07	0.2435
Debt/Assets	0.05	0.0502	0.03	0.1448	0.05	0.0276	0.04	0.105
Delaware Corp	0.02	0.6952	0.001	0.9811	-0.01	0.8987	0.001	0.9859
Internet IPO	0.02	0.8177	-0.18	0.15	-0.09	0.4736	-0.26	0.1027
Dual Share Class	0.17	0.1789	-0.05	0.7545	0.19	0.138	-0.01	0.9642
Lockup length	-0.0002	0.3268	-0.0002	0.2163	-0.0003	0.1981	-0.0003	0.1037
Book/Market	0.25	0.1087	0.70	0.0135	0.27	0.0848	0.63	0.0286
Intercept	-0.23	0.1317	-0.29	0.0647	-0.36	0.0446	-0.27	0.1027
Years	Yes		Yes		Yes		Yes	
Industry	Yes		Yes		Yes		Yes	
Adj R^2	5.5%	<.0001	7.9%	<.0001	5.1%	<.0001	7.5%	<.0001

Table VII. Frequency Reason for Delisting

Panel A. SB-2 IPOs				
Status	Frequency	Percent	Cumulative Frequency	Cumulative Percent
Active	259	48.9	259	48.9
Merge	77	14.5	336	63.4
Liquidate	0	0.0	336	63.4
Delist	194	36.6	530	100

Panel B. S-1 IPOs (Pooled)				
Status	Frequency	Percent	Cumulative Frequency	Cumulative Percent
Active	663	52.6	663	52.6
Merge	388	30.8	1051	83.4
Liquidate	4	0.3	1055	83.7
Delist	205	16.3	1260	100

Panel C. S-1 IPOs (Pair-Matched)				
Status	Frequency	Percent	Cumulative Frequency	Cumulative Percent
Active	286	55.2	286	55.2
Merge	141	27.2	427	82.4
Liquidate	0	0.0	427	82.4
Delist	91	17.6	518	100

determine outcome. Panel A shows 259 (48.9%) of the SB-2 firms still actively trading (CRSP delist code 100) after five years, compared to 663 (52.6%) of the pooled S-1 firms (Panel B), and 286 (55.2%) for the pair-matched sample (Panel C). Nearly one-third, 30.8% (27.2% using pair-matched), of the S-1 firms merged with other companies (delist codes 200–261), compared to only 14.5% of the SB-2 firms. In contrast, only 16.3% (17.6% pair-matched) of the S-1 companies were delisted by the current exchange because of unmet standards (delist codes 550–587), compared to 36.6% of the SB-2 companies. Examples of unmet standards include the security's price falling below an acceptable level, insufficient assets, and not meeting the exchange's financial guidelines.

If we consider the top two rows in each panel of Table VII to indicate success (active or merge) and the bottom two rows to indicate failure (liquidate or delist), then SB-2 IPOs have a 63.4% success rate whereas S-1 IPOs have 83.4% pooled and 82.4% pair-matched success rates. The chi-square *z*-statistic difference in frequencies is statistically significant at the 1% level.[6]

Our final hypothesis, H4, addresses IPO hot issues markets and states that SB-2 IPOs have significant market cycles which are more volatile than S-1 IPOs. "Hot IPO markets" are periods of either a) large numbers of IPOs or b) high underpricing. We begin our hot market analysis by charting the annual frequencies of IPOs (Figures I and II). In Figure I, we compare the SB-2 sample to the S-1 pooled sample to capture the volume of small S-1 IPOs in general. The figure reveals two main spikes (1996 and 1999) for S-1 IPOs, along with smaller spikes in 2004 and 2007. The lower line on the figure, depicting SB-2, shows one spike in 1996, but none thereafter. Casual inspection thus suggests that S-1 IPOs experience a stronger IPO market cycle effect. In fact, the graph for the volume of SB-2 IPOs seems to suggest the legislature was a fad that was most popular in 1996, as opposed to displaying true hot markets cycling.

Figure I. Number of IPOs by Year (Pooled S-1 Sample)

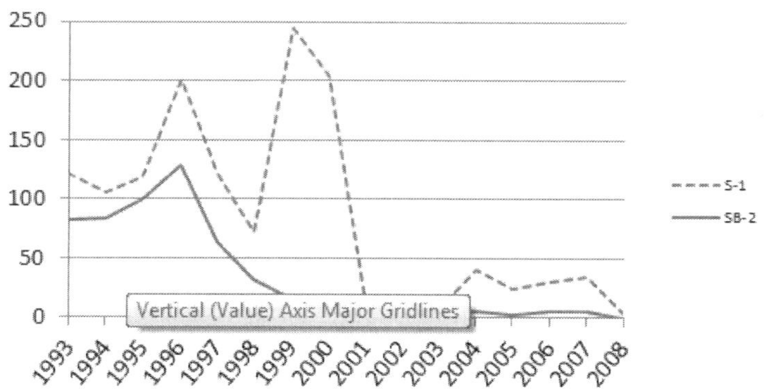

---

[6] We also compute parametric *t*-statistic difference in means and nonparametric Wilcoxon rank tests. The *p*-value for every test is less than 0.0001.

Figure II. Number of IPOs by Year (Pair-Matched S-1 Sample)

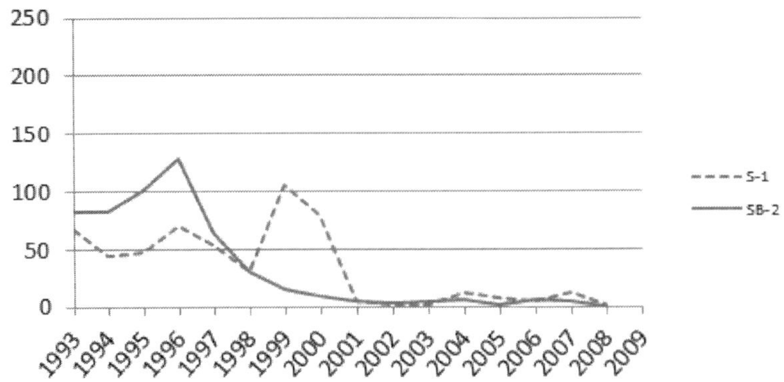

The hot markets literature uses not only the number of IPOs, but also the degree of underpricing to measure hot markets (Lowry and Schwert (2002)). Figure III charts the underpricing of the SB-2 sample compared to the pooled S-1 sample, and Figure IV charts the pair-matched S-1s. Note in both figures that both SB-2 and S-1 IPOs demonstrate cycles. The cycles are slightly more pronounced in Figure IV, with each type of IPO experiencing four peaks. Interestingly, only the 1999 peak coincides for both issue types. The underpricing hot issue market seems to be issue-type dependent and not an artifact of general market conditions.

Figure III. Underpricing of IPOs by Year (Pooled S-1 Sample)

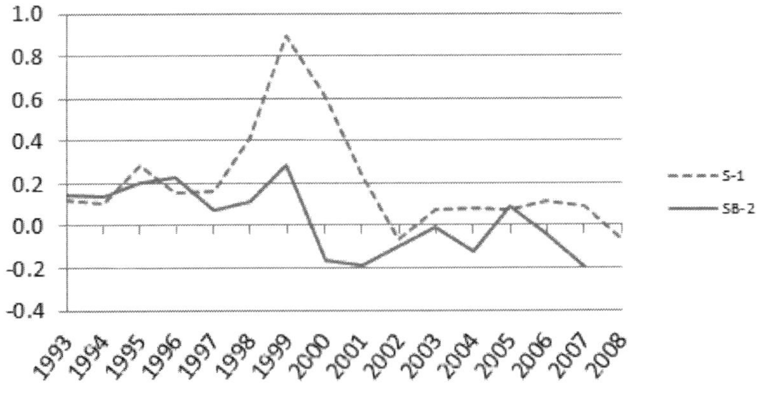

Next, we estimate the volatility of the number of IPOs by year to test the volatility of the two samples. The S-1 pooled sample has a standard deviation of 78.8 compared to an SB-2 standard deviation of 42.5. The difference between the two is significant beyond the 1% level. The number of S-1 IPOs is more volatile than the number of SB-2 IPOs.

Figure IV. Underpricing of IPOs by Year (Pair-Matched S-1 Sample)

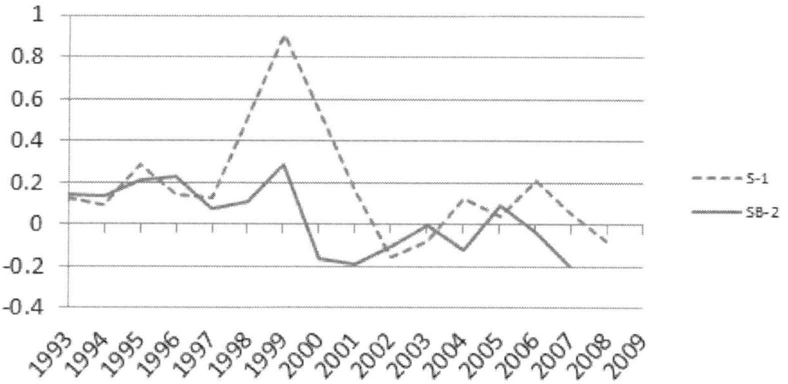

Examining the standard deviations of annual underpricing, the SB-2 sample experiences a standard deviation of 15.8% compared to 24.7% (pooled) and 26.8% (pair-matched). These differences are statistically different beyond the one percent level. The underpricing of S-1 IPOs is more volatile than the underpricing of SB-2 IPOs.

As a final examination, we compute a chi-square test comparing the frequency distribution in the number of IPOs for the SB-2 sample versus both S-1 IPO samples. Both chi-square tests indicate a statistically significant difference in frequencies beyond the one percent level. In sum, we confirm our initial hypothesis that SB-2 and S-1 IPOs experience hot markets; however, SB-1 IPOs are more volatile in terms of number of IPOs and underpricing than SB-2 IPOs.

IV. CONCLUSION

Our paper examines the three IPO phenomena of initial returns, long-run returns, and hot issue markets. We find that SB-2 IPOs have less underpricing than S-1 IPOs. This result is surprising, as many of the measures of uncertainty indicated that SB-2 IPOs may be more risky than S-1 IPOs. Abnormal one-year returns indicate that SB-2 IPOs do not underperform S-1 IPOs, and in some specifications even significantly outperform S-1 IPOs. Again, these returns results are surprising considering the earlier tests which indicated SB-2 IPOs may be of lower quality vis-à-vis S-1 IPOs.

We also document that SB-2 IPOs experience hot markets, especially when measured by underpricing. Surprisingly, SB-2 IPOs are less volatile than S-1 IPOs in terms of both numbers of IPOs issued per year and underpricing per year.

Finally, we document additional support for the small-firm uniqueness hypothesis, namely that small firms are different from large firms along many dimensions. Our use of the SB-2 program adds another unique methodology to the extant literature, allowing us to statistically test if small firms differ from larger firms.

REFERENCES

Ang, James S., 1991, "Small Business Uniqueness and the Theory of Financial Management", *Journal of Small Business Finance* 1, 1–13.

Barber, Brad M., and John D. Lyon, 1997, "Detecting Long-Run Abnormal Stock Returns: The Empirical Power and Specification of Test Statistics", *Journal of Financial Economics* 43, 341–372.

Bradley, Daniel J., and Bradford D. Jordan, 2002, "Partial Adjustment to Public Information and IPO Underpricing", *Journal of Financial and Quantitative Analysis*, 37, 595–616.

Bradley, Daniel J., John W. Cooney, Steven D. Dolvin, and Bradford D. Jordan, 2006, "Penny Stock IPOs", *Financial Management* 35, 5.

Brau, James C., and Gardner Gee, 2010, "Micro-IPOs: An Analysis of the Small Corporate Offering Registration (SCOR) Procedure with National Data", *Journal of Entrepreneurial Finance*, 14, 69–89.

Brau, James C., and J. Troy Carpenter, 2012a, "Small-Firm Uniqueness and Signaling Theory", *Journal of Business Economics and Finance*, 1, 50-63.

Brau, James C., and J. Troy Carpenter, 2012b, "Efficacy of the 1992 Small Business Incentive Act", *Journal of Financial Economic Policy*, 4, 204-217.

Brau, James C., and Jerome S. Osteryoung, 2001, "The Determinants of Successful Micro-IPOs: An Analysis of Issues Made Under the Small Corporate Offering Registration (SCOR) Procedure", *Journal of Small Business Management* 39, 209–227.

Brau, James C., Richard A. Brown, and Jerome S. Osteryoung, 2004, "Do Venture Capitalists Add Value to Small Manufacturing Firms? An Empirical Analysis of

Venture and Nonventure Capital-Backed Initial Public Offerings", *Journal of Small Business Management* 42, 78–92.

Bruton, Garry D., Salim Chahine, and Igor Filatotchev, 2009, "Founders, Private Equity Investors, and Underpricing in Entrepreneurial IPOs," *Entrepreneurship: Theory & Practice* 33, 909–928.

Chen, Hsuan-Chi, and Jay R. Ritter, 2000, "The Seven Percent Solution", *Journal of Finance* 55, 1105–1131.

Daily, Catherine M., S. Trevis Certo, Dan. R Dalton, and Rungpen Roengpitya, 2003, "IPO Underpricing: A Meta-Analysis and Research Synthesis", *Entrepreneurship: Theory & Practice* 27, 271–295.

Field, Laura Casares, and Gordon Hanka, 2001, "The Expiration of IPO Share Lockups", *Journal of Finance* 56, 471–500.

Ibbotson, Roger G., 1975, "Price Performance of Common Stock New Issues", *Journal of Financial Economics* 2, 235–272.

Ibbotson, Roger G., and Jeffrey F. Jaffe, 1975, "'Hot Issue' Markets", *Journal of Finance* 30, 1027–1042.

Kahle, Kathleen, and Ralph A. Walking, 1996, "The Impact of Industry Classifications on Financial Research", *Journal of Financial and Quantitative Analysis*, 3 309–335.

Loughran, Tim, and Jay R. Ritter, 1995, "The New Issues Puzzle", *Journal of Finance* 50, 23–51.

Logue, Dennis E., 1973, "Premia on Unseasoned Equity Issues", *Journal of Economics and Business* 25, 133–141.

Lowry, Michelle, and G. William Schwert, 2002, "IPO Market Cycles: Bubbles or Sequential Learning?" *Journal of Finance*, 57, 1171–1200.

Mcconaughy, Daniel L., Manjeet S. Dhatt, and Yong H. Kim, 1995, "Agency Costs, Market Discipline and Market Timing: Evidence from Post-IPO Operating Performance", *Entrepreneurship: Theory & Practice*, 20, 43–57.

Purnanandam, Amiyatosh K., and Bhaskaran Swaminathan, 2004, "Are IPOs Really Underpriced?" *Review of Financial Studies*, 17, 811–848.

Ritter, Jay R., 1984, "The 'Hot Issue' Market of 1980", *Journal of Business*, 57, 215–240.

Ritter, Jay R., 1991, "The Long-Run Performance of Initial Public Offerings", *Journal of Finance* 46, 3–27.

Timmons, Jeffry A., and Spinelli, Stephen, 2007, *New Venture Creation: Entrepreneurship for the 21st Century*, 7th Edition, McGraw-Hill Irwin, New York.

APPENDIX A: Variable Definitions

Big Six	Dummy variable that indicates a company used one of the big six auditors at the time of the IPO (Arther Andersen, Coopers & Lybrand, Deloitte & Touche, Ernst & Young, KPMG, or PricewaterhouseCoopers. If a "big 6" auditor was used, this variable is assigned a '1' value, if not, it is assigned a '0'. This variable is derived from the "*auditor1*" variable in the SDC data.
Book/Market	Book to market ratio taken from Compustat's common equity and CRSP's outstanding shares and price to calculate the market value.
Cash Flow	Inflation adjusted Compustat "*OANCF – Operating Activities Net Cash Flow*" data item.
Debt/Assets	Calculated from Compustat "*DLTT – Long-Term Debt Total*" divided by Compustat "*AT – Assets Total*".
Delaware Corp	Dummy variable that indicates a company filed its IPO in the state of Delaware. Assigned the value of "1" if the IPO was filed in Delaware, "0" if not.
Dual Share Class	Dummy indicating if the firm had dual-class shares. Derived from Jay Ritter's list of 591 IPOs with multiple share classes outstanding (http://bear.warrington.ufl.edu/ritter/dual-class-ipo.htm). This variable is assigned a value of "1" if the IPO involved dual-class shares, "0" if not.
Exchange	The exchange where the IPO is listed. Taken from the SDC variable name "*exchlisted*".
Internet IPO	Dummy variable that indicates if the firm filing an IPO is an internet company. Taken from Jay Ritter's list of internet IPOs (http://bear.warrington.ufl.edu/ritter/ipodata.htm). Loughran and Ritter (2004) shows that the internet bubble during 1999-2000 had a dramatic effect on IPO underpricing. This variable is assigned a value of "1" if the company is an internet IPO, "0" if it is not.
Lockup Length	Period of time following the IPO which insiders cannot sell company shares. This variable comes from the "*lockupdays*" variable in the

	SDC data.
Log(Age)	The "*age*" variable is the number of years from the founding of the company to the time of the IPO. Taken from Jay Ritter's data set that includes founding dates for over 9,000 firms going public in the U.S. during 1975 to 2009 (http://bear.warrington.ufl.edu/ritter/FoundingDates.htm). We use the log of "*age*" in our models.
Log(Sales)	This variable is taken from Compustat's "*REVT – Revenue Total*" data item. We use the log of inflation adjusted sales in our models.
Overhang	Shares retained divided by primary shares sold.
SB	Dummy variable that indicates whether or not a firm filed the IPO using the SB-2 form. If the firm used the SB-2 form this variable is assigned a "1" value and "0" if not. Derived from the "*secform*" variable in the SDC data.
Underprice	This variable is the calculated ratio of the first day's price (from CRSP daily data field "*prc*") divided by the offer price (take from SDC "*offerprice*") minus 1.
UW Rank	This variable represents the percentage share that an underwriter has of all IPO proceeds in the year of the IPO. This variable is derived from the two SDC variables "*bookrun1*" which is the name of the underwriter for the IPO and "*proceeds*" which is the amount of the proceeds from the IPO.
VC	Dummy variable that indicates whether the company has venture capital backing. This variable is taken from the SDC "*vcbacked*" variable. A "1" is assigned if the company has backing from venture capital, "0" if not.

The Journal of Entrepreneurial Finance

Spring 2013 Volume 16 No. 2

SUBMISSION GUIDELINES

The main goal of The Journal of Entrepreneurial Finance, JEF, is to encourage and support research and inquiry in the very exciting field of entrepreneurial and small business finance. Examples of research work sought by JEF are listed at the end of this writing.

The journal's audience, both as authors and as readers, includes academicians and practitioners in the field everywhere. Relevance, originality, rigor, timeliness, and quality are among the key criteria used for making decision on submitted manuscripts.

The submission fee for manuscript evaluation is $100 for Academy of Behavioral Finance & Economics members (AOBF), $150 for non-AOBF members, and $75 for doctoral students who are not AOBF members. The $150 and $75 non-member submission fees include a one-year membership in AOBF for the submitting author.

Manuscripts must be sent as either Word or PDF files. All text should be typed double-spaced, using Times New Roman style with font size set at 12. Since manuscripts are evaluated anonymously, the authors' names should be completely removed from the manuscript, and the authors should ensure that their names do not appear under the Properties of the file they are sending. The cover page in the submitted manuscript should show only the title of the paper and a short, one-paragraph (approximately 100 words) abstract of the article that provides a brief overview of the paper. Authors of submitted papers are obligated not to submit their paper for publication elsewhere until an editorial decision is rendered on their submission.

The introduction should be numbered with Roman Numeral I, as in "I. Introduction". Each subsequent main section should be labeled with Roman Numerals. Subsection headings should be lettered, as in A, B, and C. All headings should be centered on the page.

Equations should be numbered consecutively, with the number in parentheses and flush with the right margin. Equations should be clearly explained in the text, and derivations or proofs may be relegated to an appendix. Where appropriate, it may be helpful to provide supplemental sheets showing all steps in algebraic derivations so that the reviewers do not have to recreate them.

Tables and figures should appear on separate pages labeled in numerical order with Roman numeral and grouped at the end of the text. Label tables at the top and follow the heading with a description of the table in sufficient detail so that it is capable of standing alone. Label figures in the same manner. Include marginal notation in the article for the approximate placement of all tables and figures.

References

References, single-spaced within and double-spaced between, must be typed on a separate page or pages and listed in alphabetical order. Place references list at the end of the manuscript but before tables and figures. Please use **APA Sixth Edition** style format for references. This style is built into the references management feature of MS Word. Examples of references are provided in below.

Example of journal article reference:

Jensen, M. C., & Meckling, W. C. (1976). Theory of the firm: managerial behavior, agency costs and ownership structure. *Journal of Financial Economics, 3*(4), 305-360.

Submission

Manuscripts must be submitted via email. The file containing the manuscript body should have a title page with no details that would identify the authors. Send a separate title page file that includes author info. Send these files with a cover letter to submit@JEFsite.org.

JEF's Key Areas of Interest:

1. Corporate Finance issues relevant to Entrepreneurial Ventures and Small Firms;
2. Behavioral Finance- especially issues related Risk-taking, Startups, and Growth;
3. Business Valuation- and Venture Evaluation;
4. Initial Public Offerings and Other Harvest Strategies;
5. The Market for Formal and Informal Venture Capital and Angel Financing;
6. Financial Institutions and Small Business Financing;
7. Innovations in Capital Markets for Small Firms and Startups;
8. Economics and Accounting of Small Business
9. Models for Predicting Small Firm Success and/or Failure;
10. Teaching, Pedagogy, and Case Development; and
11. Other related issues- including Globalization and Technological factors affecting Capital Access and Startup Process.

The Journal of Entrepreneurial Finance- JEF

The Official Publication of the Academy of Entrepreneurial Finance- AEF
Web site: JEFsite.org
Email Addresses: submit@JEFsite.org

Printed in Dunstable, United Kingdom

91343659R00059